This book is dedicated to:

Dave Chapelle, Michael Moore, Bill Maher, Jon Stewart, John Oliver, Stephen Colbert, Trevor Noah, Seth Meyers, Hasan Minhaj, Samantha Bee, George Takei, Rachel Maddow, Jimmy Kimmel, Judd Apatow, Jim Jefferies, Al Franken, Bernie Sanders, Alexandria Ocasio-Cortez, Elizabeth Warren, Joe Biden, and all the other voices of reason in these crazy times.

Why Trump's base turned into a religious cult that will blindly follow him off a cliff, and how to break the spell.

AMERICAN FA$CISM

A German writer's urgent warning **to America**

Oliver Markus Malloy

Political Comedy

Impressum

Copyright © 2020 by Oliver Markus Malloy

Oliver.M.Malloy@Mail.com

All rights reserved.

Published by Becker & Malloy

Table of Contents:

AMERICAN FASCISM

Dear Democrat,

Trump will not allow fair elections in November.

He will steal the election like every other facist dictator.

Everything he is doing right now is in preparation of that.

Trump already knows that he will not leave in November, whether he loses or not. Trump is fully prepared to burn down the country to maintain his grip on power.

His encouragement of Kyle's murder of protesters was right on message.

And so is his propaganda lie that the protesters are terrorists.

All this is in preparation of using violent right-wing mobs, a militarized police, federal stormtroopers, and the National Guard to put down any protests, when Trump refuses to leave in November.

Everything right now is a preview of things to come in November.

Trump will not leave, whether he wins or loses.

Mentally prepare yourself for that.

Mentally prepare yourself that it is up to **you** to defend democracy from tyranny.

Dear Republican,

if all the lies Fox News tells you about liberals were actually true, I'd hate liberals too. Who wouldn't?

But that's the thing: virtually nothing you are being told about liberals is actually true. It's propaganda, designed to demonize liberals.

"Former Fox News Analyst Calls Network a 'Destructive Propaganda Machine'

For 10 years, Ralph Peters regularly appeared on Fox News to offer military analysis and insight as one of the cable network's reliably conservative commenters. But he quit in March in disgust.

*Mr. Peters, who announced his departure in a blistering farewell note to his colleagues, followed up on Wednesday with another searing attack, saying that the network was "**doing a great, grave disservice to our country.**"*

The retired lieutenant colonel in the United States Army spoke on CNN in his first television interview since his departure. "With the rise of Donald Trump, Fox did become **a destructive propaganda machine**," Mr. Peters said. "And I don't do propaganda for anyone."

-*New York Times*

"How Fox News evolved into a propaganda operation

A media scholar on the dangerous evolution of Fox News.

Fox News has always been a partisan news network. But people are increasingly questioning whether it has crossed a line in the Trump era and become an outright **propaganda operation**.

A recent piece by the New Yorker's Jane Mayer is the latest to pose this question. Back in 2017, the New Republic's Alex Shephard floated a similar argument, writing that "Donald Trump is treating **Fox News like state TV**."

Even Bret Baier, a lead anchor at Fox News, addressed the claims in a 2018 interview with the New Yorker, saying it "pains" him to hear that **the cable news channel has become "state TV" for the Trump administration**."

-*Vox*

Why is the D for Democrat so toxic in red states?

Bill Maher keeps asking the guests on his show: "Why is the D for Democrat so toxic in red states?"

Most liberals honestly have no idea why you Trump voters hate liberals so much.

This is why:

You're being lied to, to make you hate liberals.

Hitler was a notorious liar. He lied every time he opened his mouth. In his book, Mein Kampf, Hitler explained how to use lying as a weapon.

www.AmericanFascism.link

Trump lies all the time because he learned from Hitler how to use lying as a weapon.

"How the Right Wing Convinces Itself That Liberals Are Evil

Since the 1950s, the conservative movement has justified bad behavior—including supporting Donald Trump—by persuading itself that the left is worse.

If you spend any time consuming right-wing media in America, you quickly learn the following: Liberals are responsible for racism, slavery, and the Ku Klux Klan. They admire Mussolini and Hitler, and modern liberalism is little different from fascism or, even worse, communism. The mainstream media and academia cannot be trusted because of the pervasive, totalitarian nature of liberal culture.

This did not begin with Donald Trump. The modern Republican Party may be particularly apt to push conspiracy theories to rationalize its complicity with a staggeringly corrupt administration, but this is an extension of, not a break from, a much longer history.

One of the binding agents holding the conservative coalition together over the course of the past half century has been an opposition to liberalism, socialism, and global communism built on the suspicion, sometimes made explicit, that there's no real difference among them."

-Washington Monthly

Be honest: you can barely tolerate me even using the word liberal so many times in a few sentences, because to you it's such a toxic word. Liberals repulse you. They are barely even human, and definitely un-American, right? You think liberals are everything that is wrong with America. Liberals are wrong, bad and evil. Evil demons.

"Trump's Spiritual Adviser Prays To Stop 'Demonic Networks' Aligned Against Him

*Paula White suggested **the president was "anointed" by God** as America's defender when she delivered an opening prayer at Trump's reelection rally.*

*White's reference to **demonic forces** falls in line with how many evangelical Christians understand the world. They believe that there is a supernatural dimension to life and that in that realm, there is an ongoing **battle between the forces of good and evil**. As part of that fight, some Christians believe that prayer is needed to shield people from **satanic forces**."*

-Huffington Post

America would be a much better place without liberals, right?

That extremely negative emotional response in your head was created by malicious propaganda lies you have been fed about liberals.

Here's a short list of true facts Fox News doesn't want you to know. And it's just the tip of the iceberg.

Hitler and the Nazis were not liberals, not lefties, not socialists, and not democrats.

Hitler and his Nazi minions were right-wing Christian conservative nationalists who hated liberals for the same reasons you hate liberals.

I know what you're thinking: "That's fucking crazy talk! That can't possibly be true! This guy is a deranged libtard!"

Well, I have news for you: it's absolutely **100% true.** And I can easily **prove it to you** in this short book, if you give me 5 minutes.

Yeah, they used the word "socialist" in their name. But that was just smart marketing, to mislead voters. It was false advertising, plain and simple. It's like when you think your cereal contains chocolate, because it's called Chocolate Cereal right on the box, but then in small print on the back it says "Does not contain any actual chocolate."

"Were the Nazis socialists? No.

Hitler allied himself with leaders of German conservative and nationalist movements, and in

January 1933 German President Paul von Hindenburg appointed him chancellor. Hitler's Third Reich had been born, and it was entirely fascist in character. Within two months Hitler achieved full dictatorial power through the Enabling Act.

In April 1933 communists, socialists, democrats, and Jews were purged from the German civil service, and trade unions were outlawed the following month. *That July Hitler banned all political parties other than his own, and prominent members of the* ***German Communist Party and the Social Democratic Party were arrested and imprisoned in concentration camps.***"

-*Encyclopedia Britannica*

Nazi Concentration Camps

"*In 1933–1939, before the onset of war,* **most prisoners consisted of German Communists, Socialists, Social Democrats***, Roma, Jehovah's Witnesses, homosexuals, and persons accused of 'asocial' or socially 'deviant' behavior by the Germans.*"

-*Wikipedia*

What we here in the US call capitalism is actually the most extreme, most predatory form of capitalism: Fascism.

American capitalists don't want you to know that the Nazis were capitalists, not socialists.

Fascism is an extreme form of capitalism that uses the citizens as slave labor, to enrich the billionaire 1%.

During WW2 many rich American capitalists supported the Nazis.

The fact that you, 80 years later, still think the Nazis were socialists, shows how well that mislabeling trick works. It's a pretty common marketing trick actually, that's still being used today. Especially in politics.

For example, **North Korea calls itself the _Democratic People's Republic of Korea_, but you know as well as I do that North Korea is a dictatorship, not a democracy.** Same thing with the Nazis.

The Nazis were right-wing nationalists, not left-wing socialists.

*"**Nazis are not socialists nor democrats despite what alt-right might say**

The party represented an **extreme side of Germany's right wing**, and the key word in its title was not necessarily "socialism," but rather "national." During Hitler's ascension, **nationalism was preached** and took hold, and **excluded anyone who wasn't fully German or considered superior.**

By definition, a political party with Nazi roots or affiliations is not democratic since it would apply to only one race, whereas democracy is meant to apply to all people, not a specific race or ethnicity."*

–Newsweek

You can literally ask any German about the Nazis, and **every last German, young or old, left or right, will tell you that the Nazis were right-wing nationalists.**

In fact, **the term "right-wing radicals" (rechtsradikal) is commonly used in Germany to describe Neo-Nazi skinhead hooligans.** Soccer hooligans are nationalists and take international soccer games way too seriously.

It's pretty bizarre for Germans when totally misinformed Americans falsely claim the Nazis were left-wing socialists.

How could Americans be so completely wrong about history's most famous villains?

The answer is pretty simple:

No normal person wants to be like history's greatest villains.

Right-wing propaganda outlets know that, so they disguise themselves.

They don't want you to know that their ideology is identical to Nazi ideology, because they know that no normal person is going to join an American copy of the German Nazis.

But right-wing Americans aren't the only ones who have no idea who the Nazis really were. Right-wing Brazilians are just as clueless:

Brazil: German embassy triggers bizarre Nazi and Holocaust debate

"Brazilians flooded the German Embassy's Facebook to dispute that Nazis were right wing."

-Deutsche Welle

Every German knows that Nazis were right-wing extremists and sworn enemies of socialists. Socialists were the first people Nazis put in concentration camps. And after World War 2, every German kid had to learn a famous WW2 poem in school:

First they came for the socialists, and I did not speak out - because I was not a socialist.

Then they came for the trade unionists, and I did not speak out - because I was not a trade unionist.

Then they came for the Jews, and I did not speak out - because I was not a Jew.

Then they came for me - and there was no one left to speak for me.

-_US Holocaust Memorial Museum_

It's gonna be a pretty hard sell to convince anyone who's not a mentally deranged racist to join the Nazis nowadays. Nobody wants to be the bad guys.

And because the Nazis are so famously evil, their name makes a great insult. Wanna demonize Democrats? Then simply pretend they are like the Nazis.

Never mind that it's the exact opposite of the truth.

Right-wing nationalists justify their nationalism by claiming that other countries are inferior and hostile. That's the basis for their anti-immigrant policies.

Like George Orwell wrote in his book 1984, dictators like to pretend that the countries they attack are the bad guys. And when you attack a whole bunch of countries, you have to pretend that they're all one and the same enemy somehow.

And how do you do that when you claim the *whole world* is against you? By calling everyone else "globalists."

Suddenly all other countries on the globe are one and the same evil enemy: the globalists! Booga booga!

But right-wing Americans aren't the first to call the rest of the world evil globalists. The Nazis came up with that propaganda trick. They claimed Jews were the leaders of a global anti-German conspiracy.

Sound familiar?

Socialists are "globalists" who believe in _cosmopolitanism_ (the exact opposite of nationalism) and a one world government, like the United Nations. Socialists believe that all humans are brothers and sisters, who should work together instead of fighting each other.

"I am not an Athenian or a Greek, but a citizen of the world."

-Socrates

The Nazis definitely were not globalists. They were hardcore nationalists and thought the whole world was a globalist anti-German conspiracy, led by evil Jews.

Just like you believe the United Nations is a globalist anti-American conspiracy, led by an evil Jew named George Soros.

"Soros, the far right's boogeyman, is again a target

When pipe bombs turned up in the mail of Hillary Clinton and other prominent Democrats this week, the first recipient — billionaire investor and liberal philanthropist George Soros — quickly fell out of the headlines.

But there's no chance his many critics and enemies have forgotten him.

White nationalists and others on the political fringes have long cast Soros as the supposed leader of a

globalist Jewish plot to undermine white Christian civilization."

-_Associated Press_

And, thanks to the antisemitic lies you're being fed, you seriously believe George Soros was a Nazi sympathizer. That's the exact opposite of the truth. The truth is, George Soros was a 14-year-old Jewish boy who hid from the Nazis.

"George Soros wasn't a Nazi, he was a 14-year-old Jew who hid from them

The 87-year-old billionaire has been **the subject of smears** for nearly 20 years, propagated by message boards and **dispersed by Alex Jones, Donald Trump Jr., Roseanne Barr, and others**

Of all the conspiracy theories spun around the 87-year-old Jewish billionaire George Soros - that he is the "puppet master" of all liberals, that he owns Black Lives Matter, that he is secretly building a new world order - the most demonstrably insane may be the claim that he was a Nazi.

That is: That the 14-year-old boy who had to hide from his own government during the German occupation of Hungary was a war criminal who sent his own people to gas chambers.

*This particular strain of **anti-Soros paranoia has festered for years on far-right message boards**, but it suddenly metastasised earlier this week when it appeared in Roseanne Barr's Twitter rant, then spread to the feeds of Donald Trump Jr and tens of thousands beyond.*

-*The Independent*

George Soros is a liberal socialist Jew, and the Nazis hated those people every bit as much as you do.

The first line of the Nazi anthem was: "Deutschland, Deutschland über alles" which means *Germany, Germany above all else.*

It was the German version of *America first.*

"Patriotism is your conviction that this country is superior to all others because you were born in it."

-George Bernard Shaw

AMERICAN EVANGELICALS DON'T WANT YOU TO KNOW THAT THE NAZIS WERE EVANGELICAL CHRISTIANS TOO

Martin Luther

Ever heard of Martin Luther? No, not the black civil rights leader. The famous medieval German preacher.

He started the protestant movement and is revered among American Evangelicals, especially Lutherans, as the founder of their splinter groups of Christianity, which split off from the Catholic Church a couple of hundred years ago.

Now Evangelicals dominate America, while the vast majority of the world's Christians are Catholics.

You didn't know that either, did you?

Catholics are not "different" from Christians, as American Evangelicals like to pretend. Catholics are the original Christians. They've been around a lot longer than Evangelicals.

Evangelicals are just a splinter group that started with a German protestant preacher called Martin Luther in the 16th Century.

Most Christians on the planet think of American Evangelicals as a malignant, violent, corrupt, misguided cult, not true followers of Christ.

"John Oliver Exposes Shady Televangelists Fleecing Americans For Millions

On his award-worthy HBO program Last Week Tonight, John Oliver revels in exposing hypocrisy, from the compromised snake oil salesman Dr. Oz to "thin-skinned" megalomaniac Donald Trump. Sunday night's edition saw the intrepid British satirist target

America's shady fraternity of televangelists bleeding their brainwashed acolytes dry.

"This is about the churches that exploit people's faith for monetary gain," Oliver announced."

-The Daily Beast

"**No one can serve two masters**, *for either he will hate the one and love the other, or he will be devoted to the one and despise the other.* **You cannot serve God and money.**"

-Matthew 6:24

"**Again I tell you, it is easier for a camel to go through the eye of a needle than for a rich person to enter the kingdom of God.**"

-Matthew 19:24

Martin Luther was viciously anti-semitic and he promoted the idea of a Holocaust, hundreds of years before Hitler was even born.

Hitler didn't come up with the Holocaust. Martin Luther did.

"Anti-Semitism: Martin Luther - "The Jews & Their Lies" (1543)

At the beginning of his career, Martin Luther was apparently sympathetic to Jewish resistance to the Catholic Church. However, he expected the Jews to convert to his purified Christianity; when they did not, he turned violently against them."

-*Jewish Virtual Library*

Martin Luther paved the way for the Holocaust

"A shocking part of Luther's legacy seems to have slipped though the cracks of the collective memory along the way: his vicious Anti-Semitism and its horrific consequences for the Jews and for Germany itself.

At first, Luther was convinced that the Jews would accept the truth of Christianity and convert. Since they did not, he later followed in his treatise, **On the Jews and Their Lies (1543), that "their synagogues or schools" should be "set fire to … in honor of our Lord and of Christendom, so that God might see that we are Christian."**

He advised that the houses of Jews be "razed and destroyed," their "prayer books and Talmudic writings" and "all cash and treasure of silver and gold" be taken from them.

They should receive "no mercy or kindness," given "no legal protection," and "drafted into forced labor or expelled."

He also claimed that Christians who "did not slay them were at fault."

Luther thus laid part of the basic anti-Semitic groundwork for his Nazi descendants to carry out the Shoah. Indeed, Julius Streicher, **editor of the anti-Semitic Nazi magazine "Der Stürmer," commented during the Nürnberg tribunal that Martin Luther could have been tried in his place."**

-Times of Israel

On the Jews and Their Lies, Martin Luther, 1543

"The book may have had an impact on creating antisemitic Germanic thought through the middle ages.[6] **During World War II, copies of the book were held up by Nazis at rallies, and the prevailing scholarly consensus is that it had a significant impact on the Holocaust.**"

-Wikipedia

"Luther's attacks have been seen as paving the way for Hitler."

-Christianity Today

Nazi propaganda poster featuring Martin Luther. The text says "Hitler's fight and Luther's teachings are the German people's great defense"

The infamous _Kristallnacht_, the night when Nazis violently terrorized Jews, was a celebration of Martin Luther's birthday.

"How Nazis Used Martin Luther's Virulent Anti-Semitism

A new museum exhibition in Berlin details how **the Nazis made use of the anti-Semitic words of Martin Luther, the leader of the Protestant Reformation**.

"They very clearly used Luther's writings that had all this anti-Semitism in them to support their cause," Kurt Hendel, professor emeritus of Reformation history at the Lutheran School of Theology in Chicago, said of the Nazis.

**The Nazis were particularly enamored of Luther's 1543 work, "On The Jews And Their Lies."** Hendel said that though Luther was not always anti-Semitic, he came to hate Jews after they refused to convert en masse to Christianity.

**In November 1933, the Nazis marked the 450th anniversary of Luther's birth with a nationwide "German Luther Day."** Party leaders praised Luther's **"ethno-nationalist mission,"** and called their movement "the completion of the German Reformation in the Third Reich."

-Forward

Yeah, the Nazis seriously believed terrorizing Jews was the right thing, the Christian thing, to do. They were followers of Martin Luther, and therefore were convinced that persecuting Jews and other non-Christians was their Christian duty.

They didn't think of themselves as evil. They thought of themselves as the good guys: righteous Christians, fulfilling the word of God.

Like most Christians throughout history, the Nazis thought Jews were evil, simply because they were Jews.

Christian Persecution of Jews over the Centuries

"In the years 500-1500 the Jews, as a religious and a cultural minority, were often preyed upon by the Christian majority in a familiar sociological pattern.

After a few centuries of freedom from harassment during the Carolingian period (800-1000), the Jews of western Europe began to suffer new indignities as the crusades came on. The Muslims were the "infidel" targets in the attempted recapture of the holy places in Palestine. However, the pillage and slaughter committed by Christian mobs against Jews on the way linger long in Jewish memory."

-US Holocaust Memorial Museum

*"The population of Germany in 1933 was around 60 million. **Almost all Germans were Christian**, belonging either to the Roman Catholic (ca. 20 million members) or the Protestant (ca. 40 million members) churches. The Jewish community in Germany in 1933 was less than 1% of the total population of the country.*

How did Christians and their churches in Germany respond to the Nazi regime and its laws, particularly to the persecution of the Jews?

*The racialized **anti-Jewish Nazi ideology converged with antisemitism that was historically widespread throughout Europe at the time and had deep roots in Christian history. For all too many Christians, traditional interpretations of religious scriptures seemed to support these prejudices.**"*

-US Holocaust Memorial Museum

The Holocaust was a Christian atrocity, just like the Crusades and the Inquisition.

German Evangelical Christians weren't persecuted by the Nazis. Evangelical Christians *were* the Nazis.

Many Republicans falsely believe that the Nazis were not only socialists, but atheists or occultists or satanists or something.

The reason why you think that is because you've been lied to since World War 2.

War propaganda is designed to demonize and dehumanize the enemy, to make it easier to kill them.

In order to be able to pull the trigger and kill people, the soldiers on your own side have to believe that they're the good guys, and the other side are evil monsters and demons who must be killed.

That's how propaganda works.

During WW2, American soldiers were told that it was a war of good vs evil. They were told that American soldiers were good Christians, and Nazi Germans were evil and definitely *not* Christians.

And ever since then, many Americans still falsely believe that Nazis were Satan worshippers, occultists or at least atheists, but definitely not Christians.

Oh, but they were.

In fact, they were very typical Christians. The Nazis weren't the first Christians to hate Jews.

For centuries, anti-semitism has been a big part of Christianity. Many other Christian countries massacred Jews long before the Nazis did.

Here's one of many examples, that predates Martin Luther:

Spain announces it will expel all Jews

*"In 1478, Ferdinand and Isabella had instituted the Inquisition, an effort by Spanish clergy to rid the country of heretics. **Pogroms, individual acts of violence against Jews, and anti-Semitic laws had been features of Catholic Spain for over a century before the Alhambra Order, causing deaths and conversions that greatly reduced Spain's Jewish population.** Having already forced much of Spain's Jewish population to convert, the Church now set about rooting out those who suspected of practicing Judaism in secret, oftentimes by extremely violent methods."*

-History.com

How could Christians be so misguided, you ask?

They weren't.

They weren't misguided by a false interpretation of the bible. They followed the bible to the letter. The bible literally tells Christians to murder non-Christians:

"And they entered into a covenant to seek the Lord, the God of their fathers, with all their heart and with all their soul, but that **whoever would not seek the Lord, the God of Israel, should be put to death, whether young or old, man or woman.**"

2 Chronicles 15:12-13 ESV

"But as for these enemies of mine, who did not want me to reign over them, bring them here and slaughter them before me.'"

Luke 19:27 ESV

American Evangelicals love to pretend that Islam is a violent, misguided religion of hate. What they fail to mention is that the bible is every bit as violent, misguided and bloodthirsty.

The Holocaust didn't go against the bible. Christian Nazis followed the bible, and Martin Luther's teachings.

"Centuries of Christian anti-Semitism led to Holocaust, landmark Church of England report concludes"

-*The Telegraph*

"Adolf Hitler on God: Quotes Expressing Belief and Faith

"If Adolf Hitler was an atheist, why did he keep saying that he believed in God, had faith in God, and was convinced that he was doing God's work?

Adolf Hitler's quotes indicate that he was not just certain that his attacks on Jews were divinely mandated, but that his efforts to clamp down on society by restoring traditional morality were likewise mandated by God."

-*LearnReligions.com*

"**Hitler was a Christian.** This undeniable fact couldn't be made any clearer than by his own confessions. Yet, I will not merely present you with these testimonies, as damning as they happen to be on their own, but I also intend on furnishing you with a brief history of the inherent anti-Semitism of the Christian religion. I will do so to demonstrate beyond any reasonable doubt that **Hitler and his Christian**

Nazi Party were acting in complete concordance with traditional Christian anti-Semitism."

-Richard Dawkins

"I believe today that my conduct is in accordance with the will of the Almighty Creator."

-Adolf Hitler, Mein Kampf, Vol. 1 Chapter 2

"We tolerate no one in our ranks who attacks the ideas of Christianity ... in fact our movement is Christian."

-Adolf Hitler, Speech in Passau 27 October 1928 (Federal Archive Berlin-Zehlendorf)

"The evidence that Hitler was a staunch Christian is overwhelming. He banned secular education in Germany on the basis that Christian religious instruction is essential to moral development, repeatedly vilified atheism, and although he often clashed with Catholic bishops over his ill-treatment of Jews, Hitler did not perceive himself as being anti-Christian, but rather as bringing the Church back to what he saw as its proper, traditional role in persecuting the pestilent.

While negotiating the Reichskonkordat, Hitler said to Bishop Berning that suppressing Jews was, "doing Christianity a great service by pushing them out of schools and public functions."

-Inference Review

Discrimination against atheists

"Heinrich Himmler was a strong promoter of the gottgläubig (believers in God) movement and **didn't allow atheists into the SS**, arguing that their "refusal to acknowledge higher powers" would be a "potential source of indiscipline".[32]

Himmler announced to the SS: "**We believe in a God Almighty who stands above us; he has created the earth, the Fatherland, and the Volk, and he has sent us the Führer. Any human being who does not believe in God should be considered arrogant, megalomaniacal, and stupid and thus not suited for the SS.**"[30]

The SS oath (Eidformel der Schutzstaffel), written by Himmler, also **specifically denounced atheists**, repeating the sentiments above[33]"

-Wikipedia

The Nazis were God-fearing Christians who followed the teachings of the same Martin Luther that you follow.

Still don't believe me? Think about it:

American Evangelicals don't see Jews as equals. They see Jews as useful pawns. Evangelicals believe that Jews are useful for bringing about **the end of the world (_Armageddon_) when God kills all non-Christians.** And if Jews don't repent and convert to Christianity before they die, they will burn in hell.

Like the German Evangelical Nazis, American Evangelicals believe that Jews will burn in eternal hellfire simply for being Jews. It doesn't really get much more antisemitic than that.

Like you, Hitler and the Nazis thought of themselves as good Christians. They were followers of Martin Luther and believed the same things you believe.

The words "Gott mit uns" (God is with us) were engraved on the belt buckle of every Nazi soldier.

A typical Nazi uniform belt buckle, engraved with the words "God is with us"

Even today, there are still old church bells in Germany with Hitler's name or a Swastika engraved on it:

Germany 'Nazi bell' row erupts again

*"**The Evangelical Church** in Central Germany surveyed its belfries last year, and confirmed that there were still six bells with Nazi inscriptions in Thuringia and Saxony-Anhalt.*

*It told the Church newspaper Glaube+Heimat that it would not reveal their location for fear of encouraging **"far-right bell tourism" - the practice of neo-Nazis visiting churches to celebrate the mementos of Hitler's regime.***"

-BBC News

If you're a Fox News viewer, you don't know any of this, because you're being lied to:

"And while many atheists make the preposterous claim that Adolf Hitler was a Christian, his private diaries, first published in 1953 by Farrar, Straus and Young, reveal clearly that the Fuhrer was a rabid atheist"

-Fox News

No, Hitler was not a rabid atheist. That is a blatant lie.

Hitler was a rabid Christian, who persecuted atheists for the same reason he persecuted Jews.

AMERICAN CAPITALISTS DON'T WANT YOU TO KNOW THAT THE NAZIS WERE HARDCORE RIGHT-WING CAPITALISTS WHO KILLED ANYONE THAT SUPPORTED SOCIALISM OR COMMUNISM

Those Nazi Germans are carrying a sign that says "Death to Marxism"

No, the Nazis were not socialists. That's just another propaganda lie to make them seem different from America's industrialist capitalists.

The Nazis were right-wing industrialist capitalists with giant privately owned corporations like Bayer, Volkswagen, Porsche, ThyssenKrupp etc. Many of those giant corporations still exist today.

Sure, during the war, German corporations were forced to produce war machines. But that wasn't socialism. That wasn't the government controlling the means of production, as right-wing Americans like to pretend.

It was simply the German version of what America calls the Defense Production Act. When the survival of the country is at stake, the government can tell private companies to aid the war effort.

The Nazis were every bit as capitalist as the capitalists in Great Britain and America.

More Than A Dozen European Billionaires—Linked To BMW, L'Oréal, Bosch—Have Families With Past Nazi Ties

-Forbes

"Owner of Krispy Kreme and Panera Bread acknowledges Nazi past

*"The German family that holds majority stakes in food brands including Einstein Bros. Bagels, Krispy Kreme Doughnuts and Panera Bread had **close financial ties to Adolf Hitler's Third Reich**, a German newspaper reported.*

*Privately-held JAB Holdings, founded by the Reimann family in 1828, forced French prisoners of war and Russian civilians to work in its factories during World War II, according to the Bild tabloid. Forced labor was also used in private villas belonging to the family, which today owns 90 percent of JAB. Albert Reinmann Sr. and his son were **avowed backers of Adolph Hitler, and Reimann Sr. helped finance the paramilitary SS force** as early as 1933, the report said."*

-*CBS News*

Hitler was a billionaire, who came up with all sorts of shady money making schemes to use his political office to personally enrich himself.

That's really what every dictatorship is about: it's just a giant money-making scheme the dictator uses to enrich himself. He plunders the citizens of his own country, and eventually also the citizens of other countries, and shovels the money into his own pockets.

But of course they can't say that out loud, so they pretend that everything they do is for the good of the country.

Sound familiar? It should.

9 Things You Might Not Know About Adolf Hitler

"After becoming chancellor, he notably ordered the government to buy copies of his Mein Kampf to give as state wedding gifts to newlyweds, leading to hefty royalties for Hitler. In addition, **he refused to pay income tax. He used his vast wealth—which some estimated was about $5 billion**—to amass an extensive art collection, purchase fine furnishings, and acquire various properties. After the war, his estate was given to Bavaria."

-Encyclopedia Britannica

Adolf Hitler: Secret Billionaire

"Hitler amassed a **personal fortune in property, art and cash worth in excess of $6 billion.**

When he wasn't plotting his ascent to power in Germany and subsequent European domination, **Hitler was working on an incredible array of money-making schemes.**

He surreptitiously pocketed collections from his rallies, channeled millions into personal accounts through government purchases of his book and secured a slew of image-rights deals that put LeBron James to shame.

It wasn't only the adoring crowds that had no idea of his profiteering; the German taxman were also kept in the dark. By the time he was chancellor he owed $3 million in taxes, according to a British television documentary. Soon afterwards it was quietly decided that chancellors need not pay tax."

-The Daily Beast

You read that right. Hitler was not only a billionaire, he was also a tax evader. And once he was in power, he made himself tax exempt.

Hitler Revealed As A Tax Dodger

-New York Times

Adolf Hitler's wealth and income

"Throughout his rise to power, Hitler neglected to pay taxes on his income and allowances.[9] In 1934, one year after becoming Chancellor, **the tax office of Munich sent Hitler a fine of 405,494.00 Reichsmarks**

for not paying taxes nor properly declaring his income.[7] *He was given only eight days to pay off this debt.[7]*

*The new Chancellor responded by ordering a state secretary of the ministry of finance to intervene, which resulted in **Hitler becoming tax-free.***"

-Wikipedia

Sounds like a typical American billionaire, doesn't it?

The Nazis even worked hand in hand with American capitalists like Ford and IBM.

"Slave labour at Auschwitz used by Ford

"The Ford motor company has been named as one of the firms using slave labour at the Auschwitz death camp in Nazi-occupied Poland. Ford's wartime German operation, based in Cologne, is included on a list of over 400 companies trading with Auschwitz."

-The Independent

"How Bush's grandfather helped Hitler's rise to power

George Bush's grandfather, the late US senator Prescott Bush, was a director and shareholder of companies that profited from their involvement with the financial backers of Nazi Germany.

The Guardian has obtained confirmation from newly discovered files in the US National Archives that a firm of which Prescott Bush was a director was involved with the financial architects of Nazism.

His business dealings, which continued until **his company's assets were seized in 1942 under the Trading with the Enemy Act**, has led more than 60 years later to a civil action for damages being brought in Germany against the Bush family by two former slave labourers at Auschwitz"

-_The Guardian_

The Nazis were right-wing capitalists. They persecuted and killed left-wing socialists.

The Nazis were ultimately defeated by the left.

The American right was literally organizing pro-Nazi rallies during WW2.

The American right worked **with** Hitler, not against him.

An <u>American Nazi rally</u> in support of Nazi Germany. The rally drew over 20,000 supporters.

Here's Henry Ford receiving the Grand Cross of the German Eagle from Nazi officials, in 1938.

Hitler admired Ford and even mentioned him in his book, *Mein Kampf*. Twice. Ford is the only American mentioned in *Mein Kampf*.

You know who else loves the hardcore anti-semite Henry Ford? Trump.

"Trump invokes Henry Ford, anti-Semite, who received highest civilian medal from Hitler in 1938"

-*The Daily Kos*

Hitler falsely accused Jews of being anti-German traitors and a threat to national security, because many Jews were liberal intellectuals and socialists, or even communists and atheists, like Karl Marx and Albert Einstein.

"The Jews are not loyal to the state."

-Adolf Hitler

"Any Jew that votes Democrat is disloyal."

-Donald Trump (video)

The Nazis literally invented privatization:

"The first mass privatization of state property occurred in Nazi Germany between 1933–1937"

-*Wikipedia*

*"Privatization" was coined in English descriptions of the German experience in the mid-1930s. In the early twentieth century, many European economies featured state ownership of vital sectors. Reprivatisierung, or re-privatization, marked the Nazi regime's efforts to de-nationalize sectors of the German economy. As Bel notes, **"German privatization of the 1930s was intended to benefit the wealthiest sectors and enhance the economic position and political support of the elite."***

-JStor Digital Library

In other words: in Nazi Germany, rich industrialists were plundering the poor working class. Just like in capitalist America today.

Like Trump, Hitler was a capitalist through and through.

And Hitler hated communists. That's why he invaded Russia, remember?

Nazis were not socialists in any way, shape or form. They were industrialist capitalists, like England and America. The Nazi war machine consisted of huge factories that were privately owned by giant corporations, like Thyssen & Krupp.

"Legendary German War Profiteers Open Chicago Office

The company that armed the German war machine in World Wars I and II (not to mention the Austro-Prussian and the Franco-Prussian wars) is coming to Chicago."

-*NBC Chicago*

"Fascism should more properly be called corporatism because it is the merger of state and corporate power."

-Benito Mussolini

According to a bonafide fascist dictator, America is fascist: giant corporations are controlling the government, and wage war for profit.

"Military spending: 20 companies profiting the most from war

The United States' position as the top arms-producing nation in the world remains unchanged, and for now unchallenged.

*The United States is **home to five of the world's 10 largest defense contractors, and American companies account for 57 percent of total arms sales** by the world's 100 largest defense contractors, based on SIPRI data.*

Maryland-based Lockheed Martin, the largest defense contractor in the world, is estimated to have had $44.9 billion in arms sales in 2017 through deals with governments all over the world.

*The company drew public scrutiny after **a bomb it sold to Saudi Arabia was dropped on a school bus in Yemen, killing 40 boys and 11 adults.** Lockheed's revenue from the U.S. government alone is well more than the total annual budgets of the IRS and the Environmental Protection Agency, combined.*

*24/7 Wall St. reviewed data provided by the Stockholm International Peace Research Institute to identify **the companies profiting most from war.**"*

-USA Today

Companies like Thyssen & Krupp were to Nazi Germany what the US weapons industry (the war lobby) is to America: Big money that's always pushing for war for profit.

"Frustrating the war lobby

By trying to block a $1.15 billion arms sale to Saudi Arabia, a bipartisan group of US senators is challenging **one of the key forces that shape American foreign policy: the arms industry.** *Their campaign shines a light on the role that this industry plays in whipping up fears of danger in the world.*

"We must respond to the rise of ISIS terrorism, Russian aggression on NATO's doorstep, provocative moves by Iran and North Korea, and an increasingly powerful China," **the Aerospace Industry Association recently declared.** *Issuing warnings through its own mouthpieces, though, is not enough to shape public opinion.*

The industry also sponsors "think tanks" that obligingly issue alarming reports warning of increasing peril everywhere. Many are run by former diplomats or military commanders. Their scary warnings, which seem realistic given the warners' personal prestige and the innocent-sounding names of their think tanks, are **aimed at persuading Americans and foreign governments to spend more billions of dollars on weaponry."**

–Boston Globe

"In the councils of government, **we must guard against the acquisition of unwarranted influence**, whether sought or unsought, **by the military-industrial complex**. The potential for the **disastrous rise of misplaced power** exists, and will persist."

-*President Dwight D. Eisenhower, US President, five-star Army general, honest man*

And that's exactly why socialists like Albert Einstein hate nationalists, because they're fascists:

*"I am convinced there is only one way to eliminate these grave evils, namely **through the establishment of a socialist economy**, accompanied by an educational system which would be **oriented toward social goals**.*

*In such an economy, the means of production are owned by society itself and are utilized in a planned fashion. A planned economy, which adjusts production to the needs of the community, would distribute the work to be done among all those able to work and would **guarantee a livelihood to every man**, woman, and child.*

The education of the individual, in addition to promoting his own innate abilities, would attempt to develop in him **a sense of responsibility for his fellow-men** in place of the glorification of power and success in our present society."

-**Albert Einstein**, Why Socialism?, 1949

Albert Einstein sounds a lot like Bernie Sanders, doesn't he? He even has the same haircut...

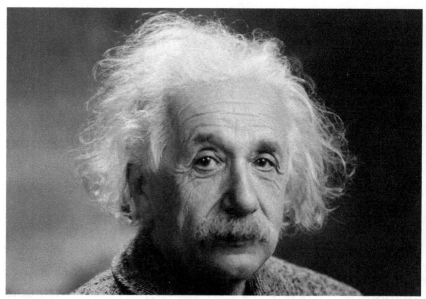

Albert Einstein was a socialist. That's why the Nazis hated him.

Actually Einstein was even more of a leftie than Bernie. Remember that, the next time Fox News tries to make you believe Bernie is a crazy radical leftist.

"I honor Lenin as a man who completely sacrificed himself and devoted all his energy to the realization of social justice. I do not consider his methods practical, but one thing is certain: **men of his type are the guardians and restorers of the conscience of humanity."**

-Albert Einstein

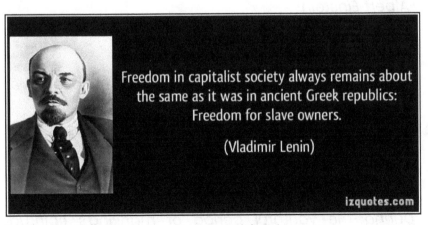

Freedom in capitalist society always remains about the same as it was in ancient Greek republics: Freedom for slave owners.

(Vladimir Lenin)

izquotes.com

Lenin wasn't the monster you think he was.

"There is, however, a somber point in **the social outlook of Americans**. Their sense of equality and human dignity is **mainly limited to men of white skins**."

-Albert Einstein, speech at Princeton University, 1948

"The word **god is for me nothing** more than the expression and product of human weaknesses, the Bible a collection of honourable, but still **primitive legends** which are nevertheless **pretty childish**. No interpretation no matter how subtle can (for me) change this."

-Albert Einstein

"**I do not believe in a personal God** and I have never denied this but have expressed it clearly."

-Albert Einstein

"During the youthful period of mankind's spiritual evolution, **human fantasy created gods in man's own image**"

-Albert Einstein

"I have repeatedly said that in my opinion **the idea of a personal God is a childlike one.**"

-*Albert Einstein*

"It seems to me that **the idea of a personal God** is an anthropological concept which **I cannot take seriously.**"

-*Albert Einstein*

"**I cannot conceive of a personal God who would directly influence the actions of individuals, or would directly sit in judgment on creatures of his own creation.**"

-*Albert Einstein*

The Nazis hated left-wing socialists like Einstein, and Einstein hated right-wing nationalists like the Nazis.

"**Nationalism is an infantile disease. It is the measles of mankind.**"

-*Albert Einstein*

Weird, huh?

The truth about the Nazis is the exact opposite of what the liars on Fox News keep telling you.

Gee, I wonder why they would do that?

Why would Fox News tell you the exact opposite of the truth about the Nazis?

The Nazis weren't socialists. The Nazis were conservative right-wing Christian nationalists who hated left-wing socialist Jews like Einstein.

Why would Fox News deceive you about who the Nazis were, and what they actually believed?

Because they don't want you to realize that American Republicans and Nazi Germans are ideological twins.

Because everyone knows the Nazis were the bad guys, and nobody wants to be on Team Evil.

That's why Republicans lie to you about the Nazis.

That's why Republicans falsely claim that socialists like Bernie and Albert Einstein are just like the Nazis.

The Republicans are lying. The Nazis persecuted and killed people like Bernie Sanders, George Soros, and Albert Einstein.

Republicans tell you to hate socialists because all Nazis hate socialists.

REPUBLICANS DON'T WANT YOU TO KNOW HOW SIMILAR TO NAZIS THEIR IDEOLOGY REALLY IS

You literally believe the same things the Nazi Germans believed. Twitter's AI content filters can't tell the difference between Nazis and Republicans.

"Twitter won't autoban neo-Nazis because the filters may ban GOP politicians

An employee asked why the company refrains from using its AI to kick white nationalists off the site. After all, Twitter had previously ushered a sweep of bans on accounts pushing Islamic State propaganda. The answer was unsurprising for anyone who's ever perused Twitter. **Content filters created to identify hate speech could potentially result in Republican politicians being banned,** *an executive explained."*

–*Yahoo News*

"A leading Holocaust historian just seriously compared the US to Nazi Germany

Usually, comparisons between Donald Trump's America and Nazi Germany come from cranks and internet trolls. But a new essay in the New York Review of Books pointing out "troubling similarities" between the 1930s and today is different. It's **written by Christopher Browning, one of America's most eminent and well-respected historians of the Holocaust.** In it, he warns that democracy here is under serious threat, in the way that German democracy was prior to Hitler's rise - and really could topple altogether.

Browning, a professor emeritus at the University of North Carolina, specializes in the origins and operation of Nazi genocide. His 1992 book Ordinary Men, a close examination of how an otherwise unremarkable German police battalion evolved into an instrument of mass slaughter, is widely seen as **one of the defining works on how typical Germans became complicit in Nazi atrocities.**

So when Browning makes comparisons between the rise of Hitler and our current historical period, this isn't some keyboard warrior spouting off. It is **one of the most knowledgeable people on Nazism alive using his expertise to sound the alarm as to what he sees as an existential threat to American democracy.**

Browning's essay covers many topics, ranging from Trump's "America First" foreign policy — a phrase most closely associated with a group of prewar **American Nazi sympathizers** — to the role of Fox News as a kind of privatized state propaganda office. But the most interesting part of his argument is **the comparison between Senate Majority Leader Mitch**

McConnell and Paul von Hindenburg, the German leader who ultimately handed power over to Hitler."

–Vox

"Holocaust survivor on Trump: 'I've seen this before – in Nazi Germany'

"The first time I saw (Republican candidate Donald) Trump speak on television, I was shocked," said Eric Blaustein, of Lombard, "not so much because of what he said but the way the crowd responded to him."

"No matter what kind of outrageous things came out of his mouth, the people waved their hands and loudly cheered 'Hurrah!' " *he told me, his eyes growing more serious* **"I have seen that before — in Nazi Germany in 1933."**

Blaustein, who was the honored guest at this dinner, made a similar comment later while talking to Navy League members about his experiences as a child growing up in Nazi Germany and as a **teenage Holocaust survivor.**

As a man who's had a front-row seat in one of mankind's most ugly chapters, Blaustein is fully aware of how history has a way of repeating itself.

"This man frightens me," he said. *"I watch what is happening. ... I can't believe this is America."*

-*Chicago Tribune*

"I am a nationalist."

-**Donald Trump (**_video_**)**

If Albert Einstein was still around today, he would despise Trump. And Trump would give Albert Einstein a malicious nickname, like *Low IQ Jew* or something equally dumb... like he always does.

Hitler told his Nazi minions that Jews (intellectuals, scientists, actors, artists, homosexuals, liberals, socialists and communists – the very same people *you* hate) were an existential threat to Germany's survival.

The same thing Trump tells you about liberals and brown people.

"Nazi Persecution of Homosexuals

*After taking power in 1933, **the Nazis persecuted homosexuals as part of their so-called moral crusade to racially and culturally purify Germany.** This persecution ranged from dissolution of homosexual organizations to internment of thousands of individuals in concentration camps. Gay men, in particular, were subject to harassment, arrest, incarceration, and even castration."*

-US Holocaust Memorial Museum

Nazi Germans didn't think of themselves as the bad guys in World War 2. Nazis thought they were the victims of a worldwide globalist anti-German conspiracy, controlled by Jews.

Just like you:

"How Did the Term 'Globalist' Become an anti-Semitic Slur? Blame Bannon

White supremacists have used the term as a barely concealed dog-whistle for several years, but the problem comes when it's used in the 'globalist vs. nationalist' economic debate

The global anti-globalist: Steve Bannon comes out as proud 'racist' on his European comeback tour

*Indeed, **like the word "cosmopolitan," the term "globalist" echoes the ideology of Adolf Hitler**, who fomented against the Jews as "international elements that "conduct their business everywhere," thus harming and undermining good people who are "bounded to their soil, to the Fatherland."*

Over the past two years, the disturbingly robust alt-right white nationalist movement online has used the term interchangeably with "Jewish" to promote the belief that Jews put greed and tribe ahead of country.

It has been a cornerstone of David Duke and Alex Jones' conspiracy theories featuring George Soros and a fantastical Jewish conspiracy designed to destroy "white" or "Western" society by flooding it with third-world hordes – all the better to strengthen their control of banks, businesses and, of course, the media.

In the case of Duke, neo-Nazi website The Daily Stormer and other openly anti-Semitic circles, "globalist" is used too blatantly to be described as a dog-whistle: the word "globalist" is used as the descriptive part in the phrase "globalist Jews."

-Haaretz

Nazi Germans honestly believed they were in a fight for their lives. And he was their savior. Their hero. **Their messiah.** And their survival was inseparably linked to his success.

"Hitler Created a Fictional Persona To Recast Himself as Germany's Savior

In 1923, Adolf Hitler wrote an embellished autobiography to convince Germans he was their natural leader

*But publishing such a self-aggrandizing portrait would have repelled Germany's **traditional conservatives**, so Hitler searched for a writer with impeccable **conservative credentials** willing to pretend to have written the book.*

*Doing so would come with a double payoff: Hitler's **shameless act of self-promotion** would be concealed, while the impression would be created that he already was in receipt of **widespread support among traditional conservatives**.*

*In the book, he put into the mouth of Koerber his own determination that he was "the leader of the most radically honest **national movement** [...] who is ready as well as prepared to lead the German struggle for liberation."*

*Hiding behind Koerber's name, Hitler could get away with pronouncing himself Germany's **"messiah."***

*His autobiography-in-disguise repeatedly uses **biblical language**, arguing that the book should "become the new bible of today as well as the 'Book of the German People.'" It also directly **compares Hitler to Jesus**, likening the purported moment of his politicization in Pasewalk to Jesus's resurrection.*

-Smithsonian Magazine

That's how Hitler brainwashed his followers into being cult members who didn't care if he lied, or played dirty, or cheated, or broke laws, or invaded countries, or killed people.

Just like MAGA minions don't care if any of the things Trump is accused of are true or not. You think you must support him, right or wrong, to defeat the evil liberals who want to kill you.

"How Donald Trump Shifted Kids-Cancer Charity Money Into His Business

The best part about all this, according to Eric Trump, is the charity's efficiency. Because he can get his family's golf course for free and have most of the other costs donated, virtually all the money contributed will go toward helping kids with cancer. "We get to use our assets 100% free of charge," Trump tells Forbes.

That's not the case. In reviewing filings from the Eric Trump Foundation and other charities, it's clear that the course wasn't free - that the Trump Organization received payments for its use, part of **more than $1.2 million that has no documented recipients** past the Trump Organization. Golf charity experts say the listed expenses defy any reasonable cost justification for a one-day golf tournament."

-_Forbes_

"President Trump argues he is above the law. A thousand prosecutors say he's wrong

More than 1,000 former federal prosecutors had signed a statement explaining that, in their professional judgment and based on the facts described in special counsel Robert S. Mueller III's report, **President Trump would have been criminally charged with obstruction of justice if he were not the president.**

This public outcry from such a large group of prosecutors - who have served under Republican and Democratic presidents - is unprecedented and *indicative of overwhelming expert agreement on the* **evidence and law supporting charges against Trump**.

Simply put, if you the reader or anyone else in the country had done what the president did, that person would be charged with a crime.

Mueller reached the same conclusion as the prosecutors who signed the statement: Trump obstructed justice. However, Mueller explained in both his report and his remarks that he could not criminally indict the president because of a longstanding department legal opinion that a sitting president cannot face criminal charges."

-*Los Angeles Times*

Hitler's Nazi minions believed exactly the same things as you. They honestly believed that every terrible thing he did, he did in their name, and in their best interest. To protect them. To fight for them.

That's why they ecstatically cheered, when Hitler's right hand Goebbels asked the mob at a rally: "Do you want total war?"

They thought their own survival depended on Hitler's victory.

Just like you.

And that's no coincidence.

"Donald Trump's ex-wife once said Trump kept a book of Hitler's speeches by his bed

"*Ivana Trump told her lawyer Michael Kennedy that from time to time her husband* **reads a book of Hitler's collected speeches, My New Order, which he keeps in a cabinet by his bed** *... Hitler's speeches, from his earliest days up through the Phony War of 1939, reveal his* **extraordinary ability as a master propagandist**," *Marie Brenner wrote.*

Hitler was one of history's most prolific orators, building a genocidal Nazi regime with **speeches that bewitched audiences.**

"He learned how to become a charismatic speaker, and people, for whatever reason, became enamored with him," Professor Bruce Loebs, who has taught a class called the Rhetoric of Hitler and Churchill for the past 46 years at Idaho State University, told Business Insider earlier this year.

"People were most willing to follow him, because he seemed to have the right answers in a time of enormous economic upheaval."

-*Business Insider*

"Donald Trump 'kept book of Adolf Hitler's speeches in his bedside cabinet'

In a 1990 interview, the billionaire businessman admitted to owning Nazi leader's 'Mein Kampf' but said he would never read speeches"

-*The Independent*

"GOP strategist Steve Schmidt said Tuesday that **President Trump's "only affinity for reading anything were the Adolf Hitler speeches he kept on his nightstand"** during an appearance on "Morning Joe."

-*The Hill*

TRUMP DOESN'T WANT YOU TO KNOW THAT HE'S USING HITLER'S PROPAGANDA TRICKS TO CON YOU

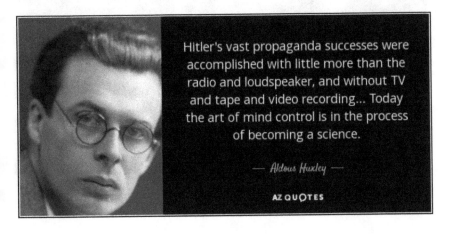

Hitler's vast propaganda successes were accomplished with little more than the radio and loudspeaker, and without TV and tape and video recording... Today the art of mind control is in the process of becoming a science.

— Aldous Huxley —

AZ QUOTES

"The receptivity of the masses is very limited, **their intelligence is small**, but their power of forgetting is enormous. In consequence of these facts, **all effective propaganda must be limited to a very few points and must harp on these in slogans** until the last member of the public understands what you want him to understand by your slogan."

-Adolf Hitler

Hitler's speeches were just as theatrical as Trump's.

"All propaganda has to be popular and has to **accommodate itself to the comprehension of the least intelligent** of those whom it seeks to reach."

-Adolf Hitler

"The frailest woman will become a heroine when the life of her own child is at stake. And only the will **to save the race and native land or the State, which offers protection to the race**, has in all ages been the urge which has forced men to face the weapons of their enemies."

-Adolf Hitler

Hitler made his Nazi minions believe that evil barbarian hordes were a threat to Germany's survival, and that the white German race was facing extinction.

Guess who uses the same trick?

"Democrats want to destroy you and destroy our country as we know it."

-Donald Trump (_video_)

Trump is using the same propaganda lies to manipulate you that Hitler used to manipulate the Germans back then.

"Take It From A Civil Liberties Professor - Trump And Hitler Have A Lot In Common

Trump's savagely divisive political rhetoric, both as a candidate and as our 45th President, closely tracks the tropes that Adolf Hitler used from 1932-36 to persuade a critical mass of the German people to trade their democratic birthright for a Nazi pottage of xenophobia, bigotry, and scapegoats.

One key to Hitler's success in talking German democracy to death can be found in the Holocaust Museum in Jerusalem, where two small green plastic cubes rest almost unnoticed on small display tables - surviving examples of the miniature radios distributed free of charge by the Nazi Party in the years following 1932. There was only one catch: the free radios received only a single frequency - the unremitting, unadulterated voice of Adolf Hitler spewing his witches' brew of bigotry and hate directly into the heads of 35-40% of the German people.

Trump's mastery of Twitter is the twenty-first century analogue of those green plastic radios, *forging a direct line of unfiltered communication with 40 million Americans, enabling Trump to stoke mass fears and foment divisive anger on demand.*

And it should not come as a surprise that Donald Trump is so adept at mimicking Hitler's rhetoric. Trump studied at the feet of the master.

*We know from Ivana Trump's now-sealed testimony at Trump's first divorce trial that the young **Donald slept with a copy of Hitler's speeches, published in English in 1941 as "My New Order," on his bed-stand."***

-Forward

Well, to be honest, he's just picking the low hanging fruit that Republicans have been planting for years.

"How the Republican Party Became The Party of Racism

How white is the Republican Party?

According to Pew Research, **83 percent of the registered voters who identify as Republican are non-Hispanic whites.** *The Republican Party is whiter than Tilda Swinton riding a polar bear in a snowstorm to a Taylor Swift concert.*

And not only is the Grand Ole Party unapologetically white, recently it has been disposing of its dog whistles in favor of bullhorns, becoming more unabashedly racist every day. Aside from its leader excusing a white supremacist murder, calling Mexicans "rapists," referring to "shithole countries" and settling multiple discrimination lawsuits, there is an abundance of evidence that shows the party's racism.

52 percent of voters who supported Donald Trump in the 2016 presidential election believed blacks are "less evolved" than whites, *according to researchers at the Kellog School of Management.*

In a 2018 YouGov poll, **59 percent of Republicans agreed: "If blacks would only try harder, they would be as well off as whites."**

70 percent of Republicans agreed that increased diversity hurts whites.

Republican-appointed judges give black defendants longer jail sentences, according to a Harvard study released in May.

Nearly twice as many Republicans than Democrats (42 percent versus 24 percent) **believe that blacks are lazier than whites,** according to the same NORC poll.

There is not a single significant poll that shows Republican voters with lower negative feelings about non-white populations versus Democrats or independents. They have become the party of racism."

-*The Root*

Hitler and Trump are fearmongers, who turn their frightened minions into disciples. They literally turn them into cult members, by making them believe that there is an evil conspiracy afoot that is about to exterminate them, and only the glorious leader can save them.

That's what the wall is all about. It's about protecting good white people from evil brown people. Evil barbarian hordes who want to exterminate you. And that's why you think Trump is your savior. **Your messiah.** Your cult leader.

"The Belief That Trump Is a Messiah Is Rampant and Dangerous

*Trump keeps his base loyal by keeping them fearful. **Through persistent fear-mongering, with messages like, "Illegal immigrants are murderers and rapists," and "Islam hates us," Trump gets to play the role of the great protector.***

But there is another important reason why Trump loyalists do not waver no matter how he behaves or what scandals come to light. For most evangelicals, it is not only fear that keeps them in line, but it is also faith.

A significant portion of his supporters literally believe the president was an answer to their prayers. He is regarded as something of a messiah, sent by God to protect a Christian nation.

That kind of thinking is precisely why dangerous cult leaders are able to rise to prominence. Nothing good can come from putting any single person on a spiritual pedestal.

When you believe that someone is truly a godsend, you can excuse anything. It all becomes "for the greater good." And when that happens, it is a slippery slope to gross abuses of power that continuously increase in magnitude."

-Psychology Today

Millions of Evangelicals seriously believe that opposing Trump is the same as opposing God.

Video: Tele-Evangelist Pat Robertson tells his millions of followers that challenging Trump means revolting against God.

If it looks like a cult and behaves like a cult... It's a cult.

"Trump promotes claim Jewish Israelis love him like he is 'King of Israel and second coming of God'

Outburst comes less than 24 hours after president used antisemitic trope about Jewish 'loyalty'

*Donald Trump has promoted a claim that Jewish people in Israel love him like he is the "king" of the country and **"the second coming of God".***

-The Independent

"I could stand in the middle of Fifth Avenue and shoot somebody and I wouldn't lose any voters."

-Donald Trump (video)

Be honest: if Trump shot Hillary, would you be upset? Or would you cheer?

TRUMP DOESN'T WANT YOU TO KNOW THAT HE'S USING HITLER'S TRICKS TO TURN YOU INTO A BLOODTHIRSTY NAZI MOB

The hatred and disgust you feel for liberals are exactly the same feelings the Nazis felt for Jews.

"Trump encourages violence against reporters, and his supporters cheer

Anyone who watched Trump's rallies during the 2016 election is well used to the fact that not only did **the president regularly advocate violence**, *he talked about it with longing ("I'd like to punch him in the face"), lamented when protesters weren't beaten sufficiently ("Maybe he should have been roughed up," "Part of the problem, and part of the reason it takes so long, is nobody wants to hurt each other anymore, right?") and* **instructed his followers to commit their own acts of violence** *("If you see somebody getting ready to throw a tomato, knock the crap out of them, would you? Seriously, okay. Just knock the hell – I promise you I will pay for the legal fees, I promise").*

Just as important as the fact that Trump says these things is the response from his supporters. *You can see it in the video: When he reminds them of the* assault on Ben Jacobs, **they laugh and cheer, exactly the response Trump anticipates.**

Trump has an uncanny sense for where to find the worst in people, particularly people on the right: their fears, their resentments, their hatreds, the things that will move them to a venomous and gleeful rage.

He proved it in 2016 when every other Republican presidential candidate was dancing around the immigration issue and he busted in **saying Mexican immigrants are rapists, build a wall, and ban the Muslims, which turned out to be exactly what the base wanted.**

When you see **Trump praising a violent assault committed by a Republican congressman to laughter and cheers,** and at the very same rally pretending to be horrified that "The Democrats have truly turned into an angry mob," you might wonder whether the assembled crowd notices their own hypocrisy. But they just don't care.

Trump has instructed them that worrying about stuff like that is for wimps. Those who criticize him or even point out inconvenient facts – Democrats, journalists – are not just wrong, **they're enemies**.

Against enemies no tactic is out of bounds. You can lie about them, you can stir up the most vile hatred against them, you can encourage violence against them, you can even assault them, and none of it

matters so long as you win. *These are the principles that every fascist and authoritarian operates by, and they have become core principles of today's Republican Party."*

-*Washington Post*

You use terms like liberals, libtards, demoncrats and *demon rats* as vicious slurs, to demonize and dehumanize liberals in exactly the same way Nazis demonized and dehumanized Jews.

"Jeanine Pirro Calls Democrats 'Demon-Rats. That's What I Said: Demon-Rats'

Fox News' Jeanine Pirro referred to Democrats as "demon-rats" Saturday, pulling a phrase usually reserved for internet comment sections and social media trolls onto prime time television. Watch below.

-*Talking Points Memo*

'Less Than Human': The Psychology Of Cruelty

During the Holocaust, Nazis referred to Jews as rats. *Hutus involved in the Rwanda genocide called Tutsis cockroaches. Slave owners throughout history considered slaves subhuman animals.*

*In Less Than Human, David Livingstone Smith argues that **it's important to define and describe dehumanization, because it's what opens the door for cruelty and genocide.***

*"We all know, despite what we see in the movies," Smith tells NPR's Neal Conan, "that it's very difficult, psychologically, to kill another human being up close and in cold blood, or to inflict atrocities on them." So, when it does happen, it can be helpful to understand what it is that allows human beings "**to overcome the very deep and natural inhibitions they have against treating other people like game animals or vermin or dangerous predators.***"

Rolling Stone recently published photos online of American troops posing with dead Afghans, connected to ongoing court-martial cases of soldiers at Joint Base Lewis-McChord in Washington state.

***In addition to posing with the corpses, "these soldiers - called the 'kill team' - also took body parts as trophies,"** Smith alleges, "which is very often a phenomenon that accompanies the form of dehumanization in which the enemy is seen as game."*

–NPR

To Hitler's Nazi minions, the word Jew was a slur that implied the worst of the worst: traitor, anti-German, anti-Christian, communist, evil, sub-human, baby killer.

Trump's MAGA minions use the word liberal with exactly the same intense hatred.

MAGA minions literally think about liberals the same way Nazis thought about Jews. They can't wait for Trump to give the order to start shooting liberals. That's the real reason why they're stockpiling guns. To shoot their true enemy: liberals.

"Trump's border violence is sick entertainment for his fans: And they love it

Trump's supporters were thrilled by the tear-gas assault on migrants at the border. He has trained them well

Eliminationism is violence, usually encouraged by powerful social and political elites, against whole groups of people who are deemed to be "pollutants," "subhuman" or in some other way "inferior." Such language and values have been almost fully normalized in America under Donald Trump.

For several decades the right-wing echo chamber has told its followers (and the general public) that **Democrats, liberals, progressives and any other group that Republicans and conservatives viewed as the enemy were to be vanquished and destroyed – literally.**

This violent language is so commonplace that when Republicans and other conservatives use it, most critics, and the public as a whole, do not take the matter seriously. It is now the equivalent of background noise in America's public discourse.

Donald Trump encourages violence against his political enemies as a matter of routine. He has targeted nonwhite immigrants, refugees and migrants for eliminationist violence by calling them "snakes," "vermin," "invaders," "rapists," "criminals," "murderers," "terrorists" and human poison who only want to come to America to "breed" while also raping and killing white people.

Trump's language is not much different from the way the Nazis described Jews and other peoples they targeted for genocide. *So it is not surprising that Trump and the right-wing media's encouragement of eliminationist violence has born lethal fruit.*

Several weeks ago **a neo-Nazi killed 11 Jewish people in a Pittsburgh synagogue because he was inspired by Donald Trump's anti-Semitic fear-mongering**

and conspiracy theories about a "caravan" of nonwhite immigrants from Latin and South America who were traveling to the United States in search of asylum."

-_Salon_

"Trump Again Threatens Violence If Democrats Don't Support Him

One of Donald Trump's favorite riffs is a wish, cast as a warning, that **his supporters inside and outside the state security services will unleash violence on his political opponents** if they continue to oppose the administration.

The specifics of the riff don't vary much. Trump laments that his opponents are treating him unfairly, praises the toughness and strength of his supporters - a category that combines the police, military, and Bikers for Trump, which he apparently views as a Brownshirt-like militia - and **a prediction that his supporters will at some point end their restraint.**

He does it again in a new interview with Breitbart.

"I have the support of the police, the support of the military, the support of the Bikers for Trump - I have the tough people, but they don't play it tough - until they go to a certain point, and then it would be very bad, very bad." -Donald Trump

-_New York Magazine_

"Coast Guard officer accused of wanting to kill Democrats and journalists was inspired by Norwegian mass shooting, feds say

A Coast Guard lieutenant arrested last Friday on gun and drug charges allegedly wanted to conduct a mass killing.

Christopher Paul Hasson, 49, of Silver Spring, Maryland, is alleged to be **a white supremacist who had a hit list that included prominent Democratic politicians as well as several journalists from CNN and MSNBC.**

Hasson's hit list includes Democratic politicians -- Rep. Alexandria Ocasio-Cortez, of New York, Sens. Chuck Schumer of New York, Cory Booker of New Jersey, Richard Blumenthal of Connecticut and Kamala Harris of California, as well as former Rep. Beto O'Rourke of Texas -- as well as CNN journalists Don Lemon, Chris Cuomo and Van Jones and MSNBC's Chris Hayes, Ari Melber and Joe Scarborough."

-_CNN_

"Hate crimes increased 226% in places Trump held a campaign rally in 2016

US counties where President Donald Trump held a campaign rally saw a 226% increase in reported hate crimes compared to similar counties that did not hold a rally, political scientists at the University of North Texas said in a Washington Post analysis.

The scientists found that Trump's statements during the 2016 campaign "may encourage hate crimes" in the respective counties.

The study measured the correlation between counties that hosted a campaign rally and the crime rates in the months that followed.

Hate crimes in the US reportedly increased 17% in 2017 compared to the previous year, according to an annual FBI report published in November 2018."

-_Business Insider_

'Only in the Panhandle': Trump chuckles when audience member suggests shooting migrants

President Donald Trump was tickled Wednesday when an audience member at a Florida rally suggested shooting migrants arriving at the U.S.-Mexican border.

Trump was bemoaning the legal protections afforded migrants and espousing the need for a border wall when he asked rhetorically, "How do you stop these people?"

"Shoot them!" someone shouted from the Panama City Beach crowd, according to multiple news media reports.

The remark drew a chuckle from the president, who shook his head, pointed in the audience member's direction and said, "Only in the Panhandle you can get away with that statement."

"Only in the Panhandle," he repeated to laughs and cheers from the crowd."

–USA Today

There is blood lust in the air, at Trump rallies. Just ask the reporters who attend these frenzied hate fests and have to fear for their lives because of Trump's vicious mob. They're fanatics.

"At Donald Trump rallies, journalists are turning into targets – and that scares me

*By tearing into the media at his raw-meat rallies, the candidate who has **promised to pay the legal expenses of supporters prosecuted for violence is all but inspiring it**. Now, as his behavior catches up with him, he's even including the media in a **"global" conspiracy** against him.*

A New York Times story late last week catalogued the "menacing, thunderous roar" when reporters come into a Trump rally. Acolytes "flipped middle fingers and lashed out in tirades often laced with profanity" as journalists made their way in.

What would it take for a rally to mushroom from threatening to dangerous to riotous? Only one spark, and Trump keeps lighting the match with incendiary indictments like, "The media is, indeed, sick, and it's making our country sick, and we're going to stop it."

You can simply say, "Man up," but let me tell you about those beatings I suffered overseas. **They didn't start with a punch. They started with taunts. Which turned into shouts. Which evolved into pushing. Which morphed into punching.**

Can the reporters covering Trump's rallies feel secure that this won't be the pattern there? It's gotten so bad, evidently NBC and CNN have hired their own security to protect their people. NPR is giving Trump campaign correspondents "threat awareness training." I have covered six different presidential campaigns, with candidates on both ends of the spectrum. It was never like this.

That scares me.

And you ought to be scared too."

-*Denver Post*

"**Cesar Sayoc, a fanatical Trump supporter with a lengthy list of convictions including a previous bomb threat**, faces up to 48 years in prison on five charges relating to the mailing of 13 improvised explosive devices (IEDs) to the various targets, among them Barack Obama and Bill Clinton, the last two Democrats to occupy the White House.

Sayoc's arrest by FBI agents on Friday at an auto parts store in Plantation, Florida, was the culmination of a week-long game of cat and mouse with a suspect some dubbed **the "MAGAbomber", in reference to Trump's Make America Great Again campaign slogan and because the intended victims had all criticised and been verbally attacked by the president.**

George Soros, the billionaire philanthropist and political activist, was the first to receive a bomb, in the mailbox of his suburban New York home on Monday. That was followed by Secret Service agents intercepting devices intended for the Obamas and Clintons."

-*The Guardian*

FOX NEWS DOESN'T WANT YOU TO KNOW THAT AMERICAN NAZIS AND THE KKK LOOOVE TRUMP

These "fine people" are typical Trump voters. They're Nazis. Literally.

The Nazis didn't think of themselves as racists. Neither do you:

"Republicans' Race War Predated Trump. And It May Outlast Him.

Their resentments are key to the party's identity.

When a political party endorses lies, year after year, in full defiance of the fact record, and its members convince themselves that the lies are so justified by circumstance as to be practically true, there is **something powerful - and very dangerous - at work.**

The alleged mass killer at a Pittsburgh synagogue is said to have acted on a belief that a caravan of immigrants was coming north, under the guidance of nefarious Jews, to overrun white people in the U.S. His action, a racist mass murder, was monstrous. Yet the belief that appears to have inspired him is only a slightly more paranoid variation on the theme described by Ayres, and very closely linked to one echoed by the GOP's white-nationalist-in-chief.

By this reasoning, the nonwhite citizens who are "in the tank" for Democrats are similar to the alien horde pressing toward the nation's vulnerable "open" gates. The alien inside and the alien outside are twin elements of the Democrats' effort to multiply Democratic votes.

In effect, the conspiracy theory about Barack Obama's birth, openly promulgated by Donald Trump, wasn't a mark of Obama's rarefied status. It's a reusable template, casting virtually all nonwhites beyond the pale even when they're born inside it."

-*Bloomberg*

The Nazis thought they were the victims. So do you:

"75 Percent of Republicans Say White Americans Are Discriminated Against

The victimization of white America put forth by conservatives and right-wing media has taken hold, according to the results in a new poll from Hill-HarrisX. A whopping 75 percent of registered Republican voters said that white Americans face discrimination.

*Interestingly, only 19 percent of white respondents said they personally faced racial discrimination, proving the point that **the fear tactics of Fox News and other conservative media who sell the myth of "reverse racism" are working.**"*

-Rolling Stone Magazine

Nazi Germans honestly believed that non-Germans, non-whites and non-Christians were their mortal enemies and bad, evil people. You believe the same thing:

"The GOP is the party of Islamophobia

Republicans were always going to come for Rep. Ilhan Omar.

From the moment the Minnesota Democrat was elected to Congress as one of the chamber's few Muslims — and a hijab-wearing Muslim, to boot — her destiny was fixed. Republican conservatives were always going to paint her as the enemy, depict her as un-American, and find some way to smear her with the 9/11 terror attacks on America.

Fox's Jeanine Pirro was always going to say Omar's religious practices were incompatible with the Constitution. President Trump, who has a long history of picking on women of color anyway, was always going to shine his Twitter spotlight on her. West Virginia Republicans were always going to suggest she is a terrorist.

Now, the ugly din has grown so loud that Omar finds herself needing physical protection.

This sad debacle was inevitable. We should have seen it coming. Why? Because the GOP is the party of Islamophobia — and it is led by the sort of folks who see themselves in a "clash of civilizations" with one of the world's largest religions.

Conservatives have been campaigning against Islam — not just the religion's extremist adherents, but the religion itself — ever since 9/11. They've questioned the loyalty of Muslim Republicans. They've tried banning Muslim refugees from entering the United States. In communities across the country - from New York to Tennessee to California - they've taken extraordinary steps to block the construction of Muslim houses of worship. Some have even contended that Islam is not a religion, but an authoritarian ideology. Over the years, some conservatives - including Trump during his campaign days - even falsely suggested that President Obama was a secret Muslim and in league with terrorists.

Omar is just the latest target for their ongoing campaign."

-_The Week_

When the Nazis used vicious slurs against "evil people," the Nazis didn't think they were doing anything bad or racist. They honestly believed the hateful things they said about Jews.

Just like you believe the hateful bullshit you repeat about muslims, immigrants, and liberals. Here are some quotes of InfoWars lies about Hillary:

"Bombshell: Hillary Clinton's Satanic Network Exposed - Infowars.com video.

Flashback: Occultic Hillary Summons the Dead, Refuses to Speak to Christ - Infowar.com video.

Flashback: Hillary Labeled 'High Priest,' 'Goddess of Occult' in Guccifer Letter - Infowars.com video.

Hillary Rodham Diane Clinton is one of the high priests, a goddess of this occult, satanic, shadow group.

Hillary 'Regularly' Attended Witch's Church, Clinton Insider Claims - Infowars.com video.

-Creation Outreach

TRUMP DOESN'T WANT YOU TO KNOW THAT HE STOLE HIS CATCHIEST PROPAGANDA SLOGANS FROM HITLER

Trump didn't invent the term *Fake News*. He's just imitating Hitler.

Lügenpresse is German for Fake News.

Whenever the press unmasked Hitler and exposed that he was not a messiah but a monster, Hitler called them **Lügenpresse, which is the German version of Fake News.**

"Trump, the "lying press" and the Nazis: Attacking the media has a history

Donald Trump's attacks on "the enemy of the people" aren't random outbursts. They have a long and troubling history

At an election rally in Cleveland in October 2016, two **supporters of Donald Trump were captured on video shouting, "Lügenpresse!"** *What was going on? Why would people who are looking to Trump to "Make America Great Again," be* **shouting a German word** *at one of his events? And what did it mean? The "lying press" – an idea at the heart not only of Trump's campaign and presidency, but of his entire worldview.*

As it turns out, the use of the term Lügenpresse happens to be quite illuminating. It sheds light on a **connection between Trump's political approach and that of Hitler in the 1930s,** *when one also heard that word used quite often.*

If the press was critical of the Nazis, the explanation was clear: the Jews. And since, according to Hitler,

Jews were fundamental enemies of Germany, the press, too, was the enemy of the people.

As with so much of Nazi propaganda, the description of an opposition press based on lies was a classic case of projection. Hitler based his whole approach to politics on lies - something he made no secret of, having described his **strategy of the "Big Lie"** in his memoir, "Mein Kampf."

Hitler lied to officials about his party's use of violence, he lied about his own past, he lied to foreign leaders about his intentions, and, of course, his whole understanding of the world was based on **the lie of a global Jewish conspiracy.** Truth would never get in the way of Hitler's goals.

Trump is also a man who has never let the truth get in the way of what he wants to say and who projects his own dishonest nature onto others. And like Hitler, he's made no secret of the fact that he lies - bragging to a group of Republican donors that he simply made up numbers to argue about trade policy with the Canadian prime minister.

Once in power, Hitler continued his campaign against the Lügenpresse. On the one hand, **he had the newspapers of his main political opposition - the Communists and Socialists - forcibly shut down. In doing so, the police arrested many of the editors and sent them to concentration camps.**

Beyond purging the press of "Jewish and Marxist" journalists, the Nazis often took over the facilities and equipment in order to publish their own papers, and with them, their own version of reality."

–Salon

"Donald Trump borrows from the old tricks of fascism

The idea that the powerful are victims who must be coddled arose in a setting that recalls the United States of today

The governing principle of the Trump administration is total irresponsibility, a claim of innocence from a position of power, something which happens to be **an old fascist trick.**

As we see in the president's reactions to American rightwing terrorism, he will always claim victimhood for himself and shift blame to the actual victims. *As we see in the motivations of the terrorists themselves, and in the long history of fascism, this maneuver can lead to murder.*

The Nazis claimed a monopoly on victimhood. Mein Kampf includes a lengthy pout about how Jews and other non-Germans made Hitler's life as a young man in the Habsburg monarchy difficult. After stormtroopers attacked others in Germany in the early 1930s, they made a great fuss if one of their own was injured.

The Horst Wessel Song, recalling a single Nazi who was killed, was on the lips of Germans who killed millions of people. The second world war was for the Nazis' self-defense against "global Jewry".

-*The Guardian*

SCENE AS POLICE AND KLAN CLASH IN QUEENS PARADE

Scene on Queens blvd., where police tried to turn Klansmen out of Memorial Day parade. Officer at left is about to swing his nightstick over the head of white-sheeted knight, whose friends rushed to assist, causing a free-for-all with two auto loads of policemen.

"The Trump Family's History With the KKK

Fred Trump, the president's father, was arrested as a young man at a Klan march in New York City. Historian Linda Gordon explains - her new book is The

Second Coming of the KKK: The Ku Klux Klan and the American Political Tradition."

-The Nation

"Donald Trump's long history of racism, from the 1970s to 2019

Trump has repeatedly claimed he's "the least racist person." His history suggests otherwise.

1973: The US Department of Justice - under the Nixon administration, out of all administrations - sued the Trump Management Corporation for violating the Fair Housing Act. Federal officials found **evidence that Trump had refused to rent to black tenants and lied to black applicants** *about whether apartments were available, among other accusations."*

-Vox

"In 1927, Donald Trump's father was arrested after a Klan riot in Queens

When he was asked on CNN's "State of the Union" on Sunday whether he would condemn the praise of former Ku Klux Klan grand wizard David Duke, **Donald Trump declined to disavow Duke's comments.**

"I don't know anything about David Duke, okay," Trump said. *"I don't know anything about what you're even talking about with white supremacy or white supremacists. I don't know, did he endorse me? Or what's going on. Because I know nothing about David Duke. I know nothing about white supremacists."*

-*Washington Post*

First American Nazis used the slogan "America first." Then the KKK used the slogan "America first." And now Trump's slogan is "America first."

When Nazis and the KKK love the politician you love, it's time to reevaluate your life.

Nazis and the KKK absolutely love Trump.

"Hail Trump: White nationalists mark Trump win with Nazi salute

*In the US, video has emerged of **far right activists celebrating Donald Trump's victory with what appear to be Nazi salutes.***

It happened at a conference in Washington of the alt-right – a radical group that has dramatically risen in prominence in the last year."

-BBC News

The KKK are hardcore racists. Racism guides every aspect of their lives.

They love racist politicians. They love Trump.

Connect. the. dots.

Is any of this sinking in yet?

Or do you need more time?

Take all the time you need.

TRUMP DOESN'T WANT YOU TO KNOW
HOW MUCH HE'S IMITATING HITLER

A major German news magazine, pointing out the obvious similarities between Trump and Hitler.

Trump is using Nazi propaganda techniques to brainwash you. Hitler was a notorious liar. Every time Hitler opened his mouth, he lied. That's how he brainwashed his minions. Just like Trump.

And if you fall for Trump's vicious lies, you are a Nazi, too. History will look at you exactly the same way history looks at Nazi Germans.

"President Trump has made 10,796 false or misleading claims over 869 days

President Trump's pitter-patter of exaggerated numbers, unwarranted boasting and outright falsehoods has continued at a remarkable pace.

As of June 7, his 869th day in office, the president has made 10,796 false or misleading claims, according to the Fact Checker's database that analyzes, categorizes and tracks every suspect statement the president has uttered.

The president crossed the 10,000 threshold on April 26, and he has been averaging about 16 fishy claims a day since then. From the start of his presidency, he has averaged about 12 such claims a day."

-*Washington Post*

Trump is a liar. He lies constantly, just like Hitler. Trump lies more than any other US politician ever lied before. And most of his lies are either falsehoods about how great he supposedly is, or negative things about the people he tries to dehumanize: immigrants, foreigners, brown people, and liberals. It's **exactly** what Hitler did to brainwash the Germans.

Hitler made Nazi Germans hate their Jewish neighbors by telling them lies about Jews. And Trump makes you hate your liberal neighbors by telling you lies about liberals. That's what Republican Nazis have been doing for years.

While you believe Trump is your messiah, the rest of the world sees Trump as an evil man, and the biggest threat to world peace:

"Trump as Nero – Europe Must Defend Itself Against A Dangerous President

The United States president is becoming a danger to the world. It is time for Germany and Europe to prepare their political and economic defenses.

Germany must stand up in opposition to the 45th president of the United States and his government.

That's difficult enough already for two reasons: Because it is from the Americans that we obtained our liberal democracy in the first place; and because it is unclear how the **brute and choleric man** on the other side will react to diplomatic pressure.

The fact that opposition to the American government can only succeed when mounted together with Asian and African partners – and no doubt with our partners in Europe, with the EU – doesn't make the situation any easier.

Germany must build an alliance against Donald Trump, because it otherwise won't take shape. It is, however, absolutely necessary.

It is literally painful to write this sentence, but **the president of the United States is a pathological liar. The president of the U.S. is a racist** (it also hurts to write this). He is attempting a coup from the top; he wants to establish an illiberal democracy, or worse; he wants to undermine the balance of power. He fired an acting attorney general who held a differing opinion from his own and accused her of "betrayal." This is **the vocabulary used by Nero, the emperor and destroyer of Rome. It is the way tyrants think.**

–*Der Spiegel Magazine*

"The threat from America

In many countries, the world power seen as most threatening is the United States.

Views of the U.S. and its leadership are in sharp decline around the world - particularly among America's closest allies.

According to a 2017 Pew survey, 39% of respondents across 38 countries consider **U.S. influence and power a major threat to their countries**, compared to 31% for both Russia and China. That's up from 25% in 2013, when the survey was conducted previously.

Approval of U.S. global leadership fell to 30% worldwide, per a January Gallup poll. That's narrowly behind China (31%) and ahead of Russia (27%). It's also the lowest score in the 10 years the survey has been conducted, and down from 48% in Barack Obama's last year.

America's favorability around the world has fallen sharply, particularly among key allies like Mexico, Canada and Germany. And that was before Trump's trade war and Iran deal withdrawal.

-_Axios News_

If you're a MAGA minion, you literally believe the same propaganda lies the Nazis believed. Trump is using the same tricks Hitler used.

The only difference is that Hitler used vicious lies about Jews to turn his minions into bloodthirsty fanatics, and Trump uses vicious lies about liberals, refugees, Muslims and Mexicans to turn you into bloodthirsty fanatics:

"U.S. sees steady rise in violence by white supremacists

The U.S. has seen a rise in violence by white supremacists, including the murders of 11 people at a Pittsburgh Synagogue last fall.

We're seeing an increase in the propaganda. They are borrowing propaganda techniques from other terrorist groups," said John Miller, New York's deputy head of counterterrorism.

ISIS inspired its followers online and now white supremacists are doing the same.

-CBS News

The refugees at the border are not a threat to America. They are not trying to kill you or exterminate the white race. It's not an invasion.

"On Weaponizing Migration

Why do political leaders portray asylum seekers and refugees as an invading army? Because it's very effective.

*The U.S. president has been tweeting about it since early October, calling the caravan "an invasion"of "gang members" and "unknown Middle Easterners" (synonymous, in his mind, to terrorists, it appears) that may be supported by Democratic donor **George Soros**, though he also admits **he has no proof of any of these claims**.*

*There is, in other words, no migration crisis afoot. There is, however, an election, and the caravan has provided a TV-friendly way to illustrate Trump's issue of choice: his nativist conviction that immigrants represent the gravest threat to the nation. **Drumming up fear about the caravan might push his supporters to the polls.**"*

–CityLab

Trump likes to pretend that all the hatred he incites against immigrants isn't racist or fascist. No, no. They're just "concerned citizens" who want to uphold the law. You know, they're only against *illegal* immigrants, not *legal* ones.

But that's just another one of Trump's endless lies. He talks just as much shit about legal immigrants.

"The US president made the false claim that foreign countries send the "worst of the worst" to America through the green card immigration lottery system.

"They come in by lottery. They give us their **worst people.** *They put 'em in a bin but in his hand, when he's pickin' 'em, is really* **the worst of the worst.** *'Congratulations, you're going to the United States, it's OK.' What a system, lottery system."*

In fact the US Department of State – not the foreign countries the applicants come from – chooses who has been accepted by the lottery.

–*The Guardian*

"Trump Calls Americans Who Came Here Through Visa Lottery 'Horrendous'

The man began his career in conservative politics by **denying the Americanness of the first black president, and launched his presidential campaign by deriding Mexican-American immigrants as a pack of drug-dealing rapists** *(with a few good people, he assumed, sprinkled in between).*

Throughout his campaign, Trump tacitly revealed that he does not consider nonwhite U.S. citizens fully American, as when **he referred to a native-born federal judge as a "Mexican."**

And in arguing for restricting family reunification (i.e. "chain migration"), the president has never expressed sympathy for the American citizens who wish to bring their brothers, sisters, or parents to this county through that program (a group of citizens that appears to include his own wife).

Instead, in his remarks to Congress last month, **Trump implied that the people who benefit from "chain migration" are not Americans at all**; *baselessly suggested that Americans who came to this country through chain migration are disproportionately terrorists; and argued that such immigrants pose a threat to "our future" - a claim he neither elaborated on nor explained.*

"Lottery, think of the lottery. You have a country, they put names in, you think they're giving us their good people?" Trump asked rhetorically. "So we pick out people, then **they turn out to be horrendous** *and we don't understand why."*

This is, of course, not how the diversity visa lottery works.

–New York Magazine

"Trump's Really Scary Explanation Of How The 'Worst People' Can Come To The U.S. Isn't True

No, foreign leaders can't use the diversity visa lottery to send their "worst of the worst" – regardless of what the president claims

President Donald Trump on Friday accused foreign nations of manipulating a visa lottery program to send the United States their "worst of the worst" – **a complete misrepresentation of how the State Department's program actually works.**

In fact, foreign leaders have zero control over the entrants or the winners of the diversity lottery. Nor do they control the vetting process, which requires the same security checks as many other immigration paths to the U.S.

Many of those people are now U.S. citizens - meaning that the president **disparaged his fellow Americans as "the worst of the worst."**

"It's beyond insulting - **it's totally malevolent**," said David Bier of the libertarian-leaning Cato Institute. "I can't wrap my mind around the fact that the president just told the entire world that these million people are the worst of the worst, to use his expression. It's not true."

-_Huffington Post_

"It's Not Illegal Immigration That Worries Republicans Anymore

The Trump-era GOP cares more about the national origin and race of immigrants than the methods they used to enter the United States.

When the Public Religion Research Institute and Brookings Institution asked Americans in 2016 their views of immigration from different parts of the world, it found that Republicans were only three points more likely than Democrats to want to reduce immigration from "predominantly Christian countries" and only seven points more likely to want to reduce immigration from Europe.

By contrast, they were **33 points more likely to support reducing immigration from Mexico and**

Central America and 41 points more likely to support reducing immigration from "predominantly Muslim countries."

*What really drives Republican views about immigrants, in other words, is less their legal status than **their nation of origin, their religion, and their race.***"

-The Atlantic

You know what else Trump is lying about? His wall. There is no national emergency at the southern border.

The wall is just a propaganda talking point Trump uses to trigger his racist and xenophobic base who think brown people are coming to exterminate them.

"Troops do not view immigration as a 'national emergency.' Not even close.

Unlike President Donald Trump, troops don't seem to view either immigration across our southern border or Mexico itself as much of a national-security threat, the results of a recent Military Times poll suggest.

Much more pressing concerns, in the eyes of troops, included cyberterrorism, Russia and China. White

nationalists were also viewed as a greater threat than immigration.

–*Military Times*

The refugees are not a threat to anyone. There are no Middle Eastern terrorists among them. Middle Easterners fly directly to the US. They don't walk here.

"Trump administration officials admit mistakes while trying to tie terrorism to southern border

*In the days leading up to President Donald Trump's televised address to the nation Tuesday night to promote his southern border wall, administration officials justified the proposal by **claiming that thousands of terrorists pour across that border.***

Data and analysis from Trump's own administration drastically undercut that message, calling into question whether the situation along the U.S.-Mexican border is truly a "national emergency" as Trump said.

*In the State Department's summary of global terrorism threats published in September, analysts concluded there was **"no credible evidence indicating that international terrorist groups ... sent operatives via Mexico into the United States."***

"That was an unfortunate misstatement," Conway said. *"Everybody makes mistakes, all of us. The fact is, it's corrected here."*

-USA Today

"A Border Wall to Stop Terrorists? Experts Say That Makes Little Sense

President Trump has repeatedly warned that terrorists are pouring into the United States from Mexico, in one of his central justifications for building a border wall.

But his own government's assessments conclude that Mr. Trump has seriously overstated the threat. And **counterterrorism officials and experts said there had never been a case of a known terrorist sneaking into the country through open areas of the southwest border.**

-New York Times

The refugees at the southern border are mostly families, desperate women, and crying children.

That's why there are now thousands of children in American concentration camps. They're being kept in cages, in overcrowded private prisons that make huge profits by locking up innocent children under inhumane conditions.

"An Expert on Concentration Camps Says That's Exactly What the U.S. Is Running at the Border

"We have what I would call a concentration camp system," Pitzer says, "and the definition of that in my book is, mass detention of civilians without trial."

Concentration camps in general have always been designed – at the most basic level – to separate one group of people from another group. Usually, because the majority group, or the creators of the camp, deem the people they're putting in it to be dangerous or undesirable in some way."

-Esquire Magazine

"For Private Prisons, Detaining Immigrants Is Big Business

A surging inmate population in the 1980s led to a boom in for-profit prisons. Today, privately run prisons have become the government's default detention centers for undocumented migrants.

-New York Times

"Trump administration to lift limit on how long migrant families can be detained

*The Trump administration will announce on Wednesday that it intends to hold migrant families in detention for the duration of their immigration proceedings, **with no limit on the time they can be detained**, according to several Department of Homeland Security officials who briefed reporters.*

-MSNBC

 **Jessica Valenti** ✓
@JessicaValenti
(Follow) ⌄

Arguing over the details of what precisely constitutes a concentration camp is a pretty good sign that we are fucked

12:20 PM - 18 Jun 2019

5,542 Retweets 26,335 Likes

♡ 81   ⬆ 5.5K   ♡ 26K   ✉

TRUMP DOESN'T WANT YOU TO KNOW THAT HE'S PERSECUTING CHRISTIANS

More and more children keep dying in US custody. That never happened under Obama.

"Why are migrant children dying in U.S. custody?

At least seven children are known to have died in immigration custody since last year, after almost a decade in which no child reportedly died while in the custody of U.S. Customs and Border Protection.

The string of cases continue to raise questions around the conditions in which migrant children are being kept"

-NBC News

Nobody likes to abandon their home and walk a thousand miles through danger, towards an unknown future. That is not a journey anyone makes lightly. Especially not with a baby on your arm. These desperate people are coming here because they need our help, not because they are a threat.

It's every real Christian's duty to help them.

"Welcome Christ present in migrants and refugees, pope urges

Even if Christians struggle to recognize him with his "torn clothes (and) dirty feet," **Jesus is present in the migrants and refugees who seek safety and a dignified life in a new land**, *Pope Francis said.*

*If Jesus' words, "**Whatever you did for one of these least brothers of mine, you did for me**," are true, the pope said, then "we must begin to thank those who give us the opportunity for this encounter, namely, the 'others' who knock on our doors, giving us the possibility to overcome our fears in order to encounter, welcome and assist Jesus in person."*

-National Catholic Reporter

Coincidentally, helping the needy and downtrodden is also every bleeding-heart socialist's prime directive, as Albert Einstein explained to you a few minutes ago.

Democratic socialism is about giving, not taking. It's about being social, and being kind to each other. Real

Christians and democratic socialists <u>agree on a lot of things</u>:

40 *"The King will reply, 'Truly I tell you,* **whatever you did for one of the least of these brothers and sisters of mine, you did for me.**'

41 *"Then he will say to those on his left, 'Depart from me, you who are cursed, into the eternal fire prepared for the devil and his angels.*

42 *For I was hungry and* **you gave me nothing to eat, I was thirsty and you gave me nothing to drink,**

43 **I was a stranger and you did not invite me in, I needed clothes and you did not clothe me, I was sick and in prison and you did not look after me.**'

44 *"They also will answer, 'Lord, when did we see you hungry or thirsty or a stranger or needing clothes or sick or in prison, and did not help you?'*

45 *"He will reply, 'Truly I tell you,* **whatever you did not do for one of the least of these, you did not do for me.**'

Matthew 25:40-45

Food for thought:

"Religion and refugees are deeply entwined in the US

The idea of welcoming the stranger is central to Christianity, Judaism and Islam. It originally arose from cultures born in deserts where leaving someone outside the city gates could be a death sentence. Religious leaders of those faiths often connect that ethic to a responsibility to shield refugees and other immigrants from violence and oppression."

-The Conversation

"And they shall wear the mark of the beast on their foreheads."

The refugees are not evil, not terrorists, not gang members, not criminals, not rapists, and not animals, despite what Trump says. In fact, immigrants commit less crimes than people born in America.

"Trump ramps up rhetoric on undocumented immigrants: 'These aren't people. These are animals.'

"We have people coming into the country or trying to come in, we're stopping a lot of them, but we're taking people out of the country. You wouldn't believe how bad these people are," Trump said.

"These aren't people. These are animals."

-_USA Today_

"Face facts: Immigrants commit fewer crimes than U.S.-born peers

The fact of the matter is that a significant portion of our society just wants to believe the worst about immigrants.

It's been well documented in studies going back nearly a century that **the foreign-born are involved in crime at significantly lower rates than their U.S.-born peers."**

-_Chicago Tribune_

But that's not what Trump and Fox News tell you, is it?

No, they keep telling you that brown people are evil, and they're coming here to kill you and exterminate the white race.

It's not true. It's a racist lie. The same type of lie Hitler used against Jews.

You probably didn't know this either, but **the brown kids Trump locks in cages are Christian kids. All those refugees at the southern border are Christians, not Muslims.** (Not that it should matter, but it's the truth, and I'm making a point.)

"God will decide if we make it

Despite Trump's claims of criminals and 'Middle Easterners', the migrants heading north through Mexico tell of lives made impossible by gangs, violence, poverty and corruption"

-The Guardian

Trump is literally persecuting Christians. Trump is locking Christian children in cages.

"Attorney who went inside Texas center housing migrant children describes neglect

The scene inside the Clint, TX, center would 'break your heart', according to attorney Warren Binford, who is part of a group of experts that monitors children in government custody."

-MSNBC

"Migrant Children Separated From Parents Show Signs Of PTSD

A government report found the Trump administration's "zero tolerance" policy caused serious mental health problems in detained children."

-Huffington Post

Let me guess... Right now you're thinking: "Obama did the same thing!"

No, Obama didn't. Trump and Fox News are just lying to you, as usual.

"Donald Trump, again, falsely says Obama had family separation policy

President Donald Trump, in an interview with the Spanish-language TV network Telemundo, adamantly claimed that the separation of immigrant families at the border during his presidency happened because of an Obama policy. That's not true.

Trump's persistent claims don't align with the facts.

The controversial family separations under Trump's watch happened as a result of a new policy introduced in April 2018 by Trump's then-Attorney General Jeff Sessions.

The Obama administration did not have a policy to separate families arriving illegally at the border. Family separations rarely happened under the Obama administration, which sought to keep families together in detention."

–Politifact

Trump is constantly lying to you. Even about the Christian children he's persecuting and locking in cages.

And like some deranged suicide cult, you're cheering for it. The MAGA cult actually wants the world to end.

#RaptureAnxiety calls out evangelicals' toxic obsession with the end times

From Trump's Jerusalem decision to Roy Moore's campaign, this week has triggered many evangelicals' anxieties about the apocalypse.

A deluge of news in recent weeks, including the contentious election involving evangelical judge Roy Moore and President Donald Trump's decision to move the US embassy to Jerusalem has quite a few evangelicals on edge.

Many are taking to Twitter to process their thoughts through the hashtag #RaptureAnxiety, which explores the many ways in which evangelicals have experienced anxiety or trauma around narratives of the "rapture." An anxiety that includes other harbingers of the "end times" associated with a particular strain of American evangelical Christianity.

Ideas about the "Rapture" are rooted in a quintessentially American form of evangelical Christianity.

Christian traditions have varying understandings of the end of the world, rooted in different interpretations of the Bible (in particular, the book of Revelation). **The narratives around the "end times" and the "rapture" are largely an American phenomenon."**

-Vox

"Trump will start the end of the world, claim Evangelicals who support him

Evangelical Christians overwhelmingly support President Donald Trump because they believe he'll cause the world to end.

Many evangelical Christians believe that Trump was chosen by God to usher in a new era, a part of history called the "end times." Beliefs about this time period differ, but it is broadly considered the end of the world, the time when Jesus returns to Earth and judges all people.

Evangelicals believe that a unified Israel with control over Jerusalem will facilitate the construction of a new Jewish temple, and set the groundwork for the end of times.

"What kick-starts the end times into motion is Israel's political boundaries being reestablished to what God promised the Israelites according to the Bible," Nate Pyle, a pastor and author of a book about Jesus, told Newsweek."

-Newsweek

MAGA is a death cult.

That's why you have no interest in stopping the Climate Apocalypse while literally every other country on the planet is trying to prevent it.

"The Climate Apocalypse Is Now, and It's Happening to You

74 percent of women and 70 percent of men believe climate change will harm future generations of humans, but just 48 and 42 percent, respectively, think it's harming them personally.

It is, of course, in lots of ways. Yet fewer than half of Americans think climate change is a right-here, right-now problem. So it's critical that a new report on the impact of climate change is about the present as much as the future.

The topline results: 157 million more people experienced a heat wave in 2016 than in 2000—12.3 million Americans. That heat and the injuries that can come from it cost the world 153 billion hours of labor—1.1 billion in the US. The geographic range of the mosquitoes that carry dengue fever, Zika, malaria, and chikungunya is spreading. So is the range of the bacterium that causes cholera. Global crop yield is going down."

-Wired Magazine

"America Is Officially The Only Nation On Earth To Reject The Paris Agreement

War-torn Syria just announced they will sign the Paris Agreement, leaving the United States as the only country on Earth that hasn't signed the agreement to tackle climate change.

In the past month, two out of the three countries left in the world who hadn't signed the Paris Agreement have joined the rest of the world. That includes Nicaragua signing the accord last month, which held out for stronger emission reductions than the Paris Agreement targeted. The other country, Syria has been under civil war since 2011 and still prioritized signing the agreement amidst the internal fighting.

The United States now stands alone in the world as the only country to reject the Paris Agreement. *The agreement even includes North Korea, which despite being against the rest of the world on practically every other issue, has decided that this is bigger than all of us and requires a global response."*

-Forbes

The unprecedented European heatwave in 2003 killed at least 35,000 people:

"The 2003 European heatwave caused 35,000 deaths

At least 35,000 people died as a result of the record heatwave that scorched Europe in August 2003, says an environmental think tank.

The Earth Policy Institute (EPI), based in Washington DC, warns that such deaths are likely to increase, as "even more extreme weather events lie ahead".

The EPI calculated the huge death toll from the eight western European countries with data available. "Since reports are not yet available for all European countries, the total heat death toll for the continent is likely to be substantially larger," it says in a statement.

France suffered the worst losses, with 14,802 people dying from causes attributable to the blistering heat. *This is "more than 19 times the death toll from the SARS epidemic worldwide", notes the EPI.*

–New Scientist Magazine

Year after year, the world is getting hotter. As I write this, Europe is in the midst of another, even worse, unprecedented heatwave. Yesterday France recorded the highest temperature ever: 113 degrees.

"France Suffers Through Hottest Day In Its History — 113 Fahrenheit

Météo-France, the national weather service, issued its highest warning level for four regions of the country.

*French Prime Minister Édouard Philippe **described the heat as "exceptional in its precocity and intensity,"** saying government preparations were not an overreaction but a necessity.*

*Some 4,000 schools closed for the day out of concern for children's safety, he said. As part of emergency heat wave plans, **public cooling rooms had opened in Paris and other cities, and parks and pools stayed open for extended hours. Parisians could also use a smartphone app to find places to cool down.**"*

–NPR

That is insane. The world is on fire.

"By the numbers: Unprecedented devastation of California's wildfires

There is a trend, driven by climate change, decades of fire management policies and human development, toward larger fires in California. **Heat is a big factor in these fires.**

California had its hottest month on record in July, with average temperatures at 5°F above the 20th Century average. Death Valley, California, set a record for the hottest month of any location on Earth, NOAA found.

Out of the top 20 largest wildfires in California history, only one occurred before 1950.

All of the top 10 largest wildfires have taken place during the past decade, with four out of the top 5 occurring since 2010."

-_Axios News_

Instead of following Christ's teachings, and helping those in need, the deranged MAGA death cult cheers when Trump persecutes brown Christian refugees from Latin America, and watches the world burn.

THE NRA DOESN'T WANT YOU TO KNOW
THAT THE NAZIS WERE PRO-GUN

You know how Fox News always says the Nazis were anti-gun?

That's a lie, too.

Nazis love guns.

When the Nazis took power, they *relaxed* gun laws. The Nazis made it *easier* to own a gun, not harder. You didn't even need a permit to buy a rifle anymore:

"The 1938 German Weapons Act, the precursor of the current weapons law, superseded the 1928 law. As under the 1928 law, citizens were required to have a permit to carry a firearm and a separate permit to acquire a firearm.

But under the new law:

Gun restriction laws applied only to handguns, not to long guns or ammunition.

The 1938 revisions completely deregulated the acquisition and transfer of rifles and shotguns, and the possession of ammunition.

The legal age at which guns could be purchased was lowered from 20 to 18.

Holders of annual hunting permits, government workers, and NSDAP (the National Socialist German Workers' Party) members were no longer subject to gun ownership restrictions.

Prior to the 1938 law, only officials of the central government, the states, and employees of the German Reichsbahn Railways were exempted."

-*Wikipedia*

I know what you're thinking: "But wait! The Nazis disarmed the Jews! That means they were anti-gun!"

Does it though? No. No, it doesn't.

In Nazi Germany, Jews were considered dangerous enemies of the state. Would you let enemies of the state have weapons?

No, no you wouldn't. That's why even today, in super pro-gun America, felons are not allowed to have guns. Because felons are considered dangerous enemies of the state.

When the Nazis disarmed the Jews in 1938, there were only 214,000 Jews left in Germany. But there were 60 million Germans. So in Nazi Germany, 60 million people were allowed to have guns, and only 214,000 people were not allowed to have guns.

In America today, <u>millions of felons are not allowed to have guns</u> because of a federal ban.

"People with felony convictions more broadly account for 8 percent of the overall population and 33 percent of the African-American male population."

-UGA Today

Today, right now, more African Americans are banned from owning a gun in America, than there ever were Jews banned from owning a gun in Nazi Germany.

"Historians note that there were only around 214,000 German Jews left in the country by 1938, and therefore disarming the Jewish population didn't have a larger impact on the Nazi's continued assault on surrounding countries. In fact, suggesting that 214,000 people with personal firearms could successfully defeat the Nazis and all who colluded with them is "mind-bending," according to the CEO of the Anti-Defamation League, Jonathan Greenblatt."

-Forward

That's a Jewish article about the Holocaust, published in a Jewish newspaper, written by a Jewish expert from a Jewish organization that deals with Jewish history. What I'm saying is, he knows what he's talking about.

Today, right now, super pro-gun America is banning millions more people from owning a gun than Nazi Germany ever did. The Nazis were more pro-gun than America today.

The Nazis were very pro-gun and would looove the NRA. Every good German had a gun, to protect the homeland against evil barbarian hordes and evil globalist Jews.

Why would Fox News tell you that the Nazi Germans were anti-gun liberals, when that's a monumental lie, and the exact opposite of the truth?

Because you're being brainwashed, just like the Nazis were.

Hitler was the first to weaponize radio broadcasts, which was cutting edge technology back then.

Trump uses Twitter, but Hitler was the first to brainwash people by using an early form of social media. Hitler sold millions of cheap radios (Volksempfaenger) to his followers. It was the iPhone and the Twitter of its day. It received only one station: Hitler's voice. That's how he filled his followers' heads with hateful lies about foreigners.

Fox News weaponized TV:

"It's time — high time — to take Fox News's destructive role in America seriously

The network, which attracts more viewers than its two major competitors, specializes in fearmongering and unrelenting alarmism. Remember "the caravan"?

Fox, you might recall, was a welcoming haven for "birtherism" — the racist lies about President Barack Obama's birthplace. For years, it has constantly, unfairly and inaccurately bashed Hillary Clinton.

And its most high-profile personality, Sean Hannity, is not only a close confidant of President Trump but appeared with him onstage at a campaign rally last year.

Fox News shouldn't be treated as an honest broker of political news.

What Fox News has become is destructive."

-Washington Post

Infowars weaponized YouTube:

"The bizarre political rise and fall of Infowars' Alex Jones

*Alex Jones has spent much of the past 23 years on the outskirts of political society, **spreading conspiracy theories and lies.***

*With the rise of President Donald Trump, who has been described in media outlets as the "human distillation" of the conspiracy monger's paranoid worldview, Jones appeared set to finally make it into the mainstream. But now, amid a global backlash against **the chaotic forces Jones helped propel**, the social media companies that fueled his rise may have closed him out for good.*

"You have an amazing reputation. I will not let you down," Trump told Jones in an interview from Trump Tower in December 2015.

-CNBC

And Trump weaponized Twitter:

"Dan Rather: With Twitter, Donald Trump Has "Most Powerful Platform For Propaganda" In Human History

This is a whole new age. And the president has the strongest, the most powerful platform for propaganda that humans have ever had. No president has ever had this kind of reach, the combination of television, radio, the internet, social media, tweets."

–*Real Clear Politics*

"He Calls Hillary Clinton a 'Demon.' Who Is Alex Jones?

President Obama took a moment at a rally this week to sniff his hand to prove that he is **not really a demon from hell who reeks of sulfur and walks the Earth swarmed by flies.** *Why would the president of the United States do such a thing, even in jest?*

"I was reading the other day there is a guy on the radio who apparently — **Trump's on his show frequently — he said me and Hillary are demons,***" Mr. Obama explained to the laughing crowd. "Said we smelled like sulfur. Ain't that something?"*

–*New York Times*

"How Fox News Created the War on Christmas

This isn't to say that Fox hosts originated the idea of a war on Christmas. **The term arose in the writings of anti-immigration activist** *Peter Brimelow in 1999 but languished until October 2005, when John Gibson appeared on The O'Reilly Factor to discuss his new book,* **The War on Christmas: How the Liberal Plot to Ban the Sacred Christian Holiday Is Worse Than You Thought."**

–*Harvard Business Review*

It's always the same basic principle: spreading hateful lies about minorities and your opponents, to make gullible white people falsely believe they're under attack by demonic evil.

The propaganda medium of choice just became more modern over time.

"In the big lie there is always a certain force of credibility. In the primitive simplicity of their minds they more readily fall victims to the big lie than the small lie, *since they themselves often tell small lies in little matters but would be ashamed to resort to large-scale falsehoods.*

It would never come into their heads to fabricate colossal untruths, and they would not believe that others could have the impudence to distort the truth so infamously. *Even though the facts which prove this to be so may be brought clearly to their minds, they will still doubt and waver and will continue to think that there may be some other explanation.*

For the grossly impudent lie always leaves traces behind it, even after it has been nailed down, a fact which is known to all expert liars in this world and to all who conspire together in the art of lying."

–Adolf Hitler

Soulmates

Video: The Trump cult is the biggest threat American democracy has ever faced.

As I explained in this short book, MAGA minions think of Trump as God's Chosen One, and think of themselves as God's Christian warriors, and liberals

as demons. Actual satanic demons from hell who smell like sulfur.

'Demon' Obama sniffs hand to check for sulphur – video

*President Barack Obama sniffs his own hand at a campaign rally for Hillary Clinton in North Carolina on Tuesday, after Trump-supporting radio host Alex Jones said on Monday that **Clinton and Obama are demons from hell who smell like sulphu**r"*

-*The Guardian*

"If and when these preachers get control of the [Republican] party, and they're sure trying to do so, it's going to be a terrible damn problem. Frankly, **these people frighten me.** Politics and governing demand compromise. But **these Christians believe they are acting in the name of God, so they can't and won't compromise.** I know, I've tried to deal with them."

-Barry Goldwater

"What is a Christian Warrior?

In the Bible, **Christianity is compared to warfare. Indeed, it is a very real aspect of the way that those who follow Christ must live. Those who desire to live this way will face many battles—battles that MUST BE WON if we are to make it into the kingdom of God.** *There is effort involved—energy must be expended in the day-to-day life of a true Christian.*

The reward—ETERNAL LIFE!—is well worth this effort. We dare not let this goal slip away."

-*The Restored Church of God*

Good "Christian warriors" don't coexist with demons. They exterminate them.

"Planned Parenthood shooter 'happy' with his attack

The man who admits to killing three people at a Colorado Springs Planned Parenthood clinic last fall told police he dreamed he'll be met in Heaven by aborted fetuses wanting to thank him for saving unborn babies, according to newly released court documents."

-*USA Today*

And that's exactly what Trump's MAGA minions want to do. They don't just want to beat liberals in elections. They want to exterminate liberals. Like the Nazis tried to exterminate the Jews.

"The Far Right doesn't want to beat the Left; it wants to exterminate it

Every right-wing authoritarian movement has one thing in common: a brutal clampdown on any persons or groups who promote equality.

"There's a growing, rabid, conspiratorial anti-leftism on the right. That anti-leftism has been metastasizing for decades, and it has a growing body count. Yet **the right's hatred of and violence against people on the left is rarely treated as a trend by the media.**

The rhetoric on the right over recent decades is disturbing. Right-wing pundits have joked about murdering people on the left for years. *In the 1990s, talk-radio host Rush Limbaugh quipped, "I tell people: 'Don't kill all the liberals. Leave enough so we can have two on every campus—living fossils—so we will never forget what these people stood for.'"*

His words were echoed recently by the neo-Nazi Chris Cantwell, who ranted in a Gab post that leftists should face "complete and total destruction."

Adolf Hitler's prejudice against Jewish people is widely understood and condemned today. But his parallel and rabid hatred of leftists is less frequently broached in popular discussions of the Second World War. Yet the two hatreds were deeply intertwined. The scholar Robert Paxton has noted that **fascism was distinguished specifically by "an anti-liberal, anti-socialist, violently exclusionary, expansionist nationalist agenda."**

In his book Mein Kampf, Hitler is obsessed with what he called "Bolshevist-Jewish" Communism. Hitler hated leftists because he saw them as Jewish, and Jews because he saw them as leftists.

-Pacific Standard

Trump shares video of cowboy activist saying 'the only good Democrat is a dead Democrat'

-The Independent

And that, dear Bill Maher, is why the D for Democrat is so toxic in red states.

Tell a friend about this book:

www.AmericanFascism.link

–

Contact the author at:

Oliver.M.Malloy@Mail.com

–

Social Media:

Malloy.rocks

Reddit.com/r/AmericanFascism2020

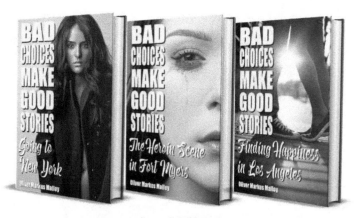